All the Women in the Bible:
Sisters & Sisterhood

Christine M. Carpenter
The Listening Lady

CMC Press, Portland, Oregon

Copyright © 1995 Christine M. Carpenter

CMC Press
P. O. Box 8716
Portland, Oregon 97297

All rights reserved. No part of this book may be reproduced or transmitted in any form or by any means, electronic or mechanical, including photocopying and recording, or by any information storage system, except as may be expressly permitted by the 1976 Copyright Act, or by written permission of the publisher. For information or permission, write: CMC Press, P.O. Box 8716, Portland, Oregon 97207.

Scripture quotations from the New Revised Standard Version of the Bible are copyright © 1989 by the Division of Christian Education of the National Council of the Churches of Christ in the U.S.A. and are used by permission.

ISBN 1-887999-66-3 (Volume 1)
ISBN 1-887999-56-6 (6 Volume Set)

To girls and women everywhere throughout time.

CONTENTS

Acknowledgments .... *viii*
Preface .... *xi*
Introduction .... *xiii*
   Why This Book .... *xiii*
   Why I Wrote This Book .... *xiii*
   Why Read This Book .... *xiv*
   How to Use This Book .... *xv*

Chapter One:
All the Sisters in the Bible Overview

All the Sisters in the Bible Overview 2
Sisters in Chronological Order 2
Selected Unnamed Sisters 8
Background on Sisters 9
Focus Virtues 12
Why Value Virtues? 13
Reflection 18
Bible Verses Containing Sister 22
   Sister: 22
   Sisters: 23
Virtues Reflection: Overview 25
Action Scripture 26
Grateful Prayer 26

iv

Chapter Two:
Lot's Daughters

Lot's Daughters 28
Lot's Daughters' Family Tree 34
Sodom & Gomorrah Facts & Theories: 36
    Time & Location of Sodom & Gomorrah 36
    Geology of Sodom and Gomorrah 38
    Life in Sodom and Gomorrah 41
Why Save Lot & His Family? 44
The Mother of Lot's Daughters 45
Reflection 50
Lot's Daughters 54
    Focus Virtue: Unity 54
Virtues Reflection: Lot's Daughters 55
Action Scripture 56
Grateful Prayer 56

Chapter Three:
Leah & Rachel

Leah & Rachel 58
Leah & Rachel's Family Tree 64
Wedding Traditions of the Times 66
Sisters Name Their Children 69
Why Argue Over Mandrakes? 71
Jacob's Past Affected Everyone's Future 74
Final Resting Places 78
Reflection 80
Leah 83
    Focus Virtue: Honor 83

Rachel 84
   Focus Virtue: Determination 84
Virtues Reflection: Leah & Rachel 85
Action Scripture 86
Grateful Prayer 86

Chapter Four:
Mahlah, Noah, Hoglah, Milcah, & Tirzah

Mahlah, Noah, Hoglah, Milcah, & Tirzah
   (Zelophehad's Daughters) 88
The Israelite Journey: The Exodus to the
   Promised Land 94
Summary of the Wilderness Rebellions 96
More Details About Some Rebellions 98
Selected Female Role Models of the Time 102
The Ark of the Covenant & God 103
Reflection 107
Mahlah 110
   Focus Virtue: Assertiveness 110
Virtues Reflection: Mahlah, Noah, Hoglah,
   Milcah, & Tirzah (Zelophehad's Daughters) 111
Action Scripture 112
Grateful Prayer 112

Chapter Five:
Martha & Mary

Martha & Mary 114
Map of Jerusalem and Vicinity 121
The Times & Traditions 122

vi

Martha Facts, Legends, & Concepts 126
Mary Facts, Legends, & Concepts 130
Reflection 133
Martha 139
    Focus Virtue: Friendliness 139
Mary 140
    Focus Virtue: Reverence 140
Virtues Reflection: Martha & Mary 141
Action Scripture 142
Grateful Prayer 142

Chapter Six:
Bernice & Drusilla

Bernice & Drusilla 144
Bernice & Drusilla's Family Tree 150
The Roman Court System 152
Roads & Travel 157
Reflection 160
Bernice 166
    Focus Virtue: Mercifulness 166
Drusilla 167
    Focus Virtue: Respectfulness 167
Virtues Reflection: Bernice & Drusilla 168
Action Scripture 169
Grateful Prayer 169

Selected References/Readings *171*

Acknowledgments

I would like to acknowledge, for their *generosity,* the Division of Christian Education of the National Council of Churches of Christ in the U.S.A., because the Scripture quotations used herein are from the New Revised Standard Version of the Bible, copyright © 1989 by the Division of Christian Education of the National Council of Churches of Christ in the U.S.A., and are used by permission. All rights reserved. Because they have been generous and considerate of the needs of others, reading the scriptures is made surer and easier by having them printed in each study section in this book. My own spiritual life has taken on a wonderful dimension because I can turn to the pages in this book and find the scriptures immediately available within the context of the writing.

I would like to acknowledge, for her *purposefulness,* Edith Deen, author of *All of the Women of the Bible,* because she envisioned a worthwhile project and focused her concentration on research and imaginative development of the stories of the women in the Bible—without the assistance of a personal computer—and it was her book, published in 1955, that was the inspiration for me to tackle, complete, and share the book that was within me, about *All the Women in the Bible.* My mind is sharper because Edith Deen, through her work, challenged me to think critically to examine and evaluate what I unquestioningly had learned so well from my teachers over the decades.

I would like to acknowledge, for their *determination,* Linda Kavelin Popov, Dan Popov, and John Kavelin, the creators of The Virtues Project, because their virtues made it possible for them to conceive, develop, and deliver a practical and timely system for parents to teach virtues to their children. Their virtues list inspired my Christian virtues research and the integration of Christian virtues with women in the Bible. My heart rejoices even more because The Virtues Project has given me tools to identify, develop, and support the good that is within us all.

I would like to acknowledge, for their *steadfastness,* the women who for a year and a half attended weekly Bible studies that were the seeds of this tome, because they demonstrated their steadfastness I was encouraged to commit to and renew my own steadfastness, week after week. The writing that I do is better because these women asked me the difficult questions that I had to research before I could include the answers in this book.

I would like to acknowledge, for her *discernment,* Jeanette Soby, my friend and colleague, because she has seen, understood, and shared what was unknowable to me. Her discernment has been both enlightening and inspiring as we have journeyed together in the material world of our writings and through the spiritual world of our hearts. This book is better because Jeanette has shared her time, energy, and ideas to make it so.

I would like to acknowledge, for his *wisdom,* Kevin Shilts, my husband, because he has let the virtue of wisdom lead him daily and has known, said, and done the wisest possible things that would nurture our relationship with one another and with God. He has given me needed perspective and support, not just for this project, but for a better life.

Finally, I would like to acknowledge that it is the Spirit of truth who has guided me into the *truth* I live by and share. As we consider and learn from all the women in the Bible, I acknowledge my *trust* in God, that the words of Jesus will be true for me as well as for you as we move to new levels of truth, daily. Gladly, I remind us all, that Jesus said that *"When the Spirit of truth comes, he will guide you into all the truth..."* (John 16:13). May you find this part of your life journey a blessing.

Preface

Please know that I am aware of the hazards. I want to do it because I want to do it. Women must try to do things as men have tried. When they fail, their failure must be but a challenge to others.

Amelia Earhart
—in her last letter to her husband

It is easy for me to identify with Amelia Earhart's words, because for me and others attempting to write about sisters in the Bible, it is often hazardous. I realize that my desire to share the lives, limitations, strengths, and loveliness of the sisters in the Bible will create strong feelings in women and men who carefully consider the information and ideas presented. While tradition says that Amelia Earhart crashed and burned as a result of her effort to achieve her desire, it is not my intention to follow her example in that way!

To the contrary, it is my intention that this collection of biblical women be successful. Success in this context will mean that the reader will be stimulated, inspired, and encouraged by the material. In some cases, being stimulated may mean that the reader becomes irritated, aggravated, or enraged by the material. In all cases, this material is designed to create opportunities to sense, feel, and react. Because we are all unique, our encounter with new and old ideas will vary, depending on our current belief system, our current need, and our current physical, mental, and spiritual conditions.

Those individuals who will benefit most by this material will be those who react to it—in any way! So, relax and enjoy the experience of visiting or revisiting some of our sisters in the Bible. I believe it is a risk worth taking, a challenge worth making, a Giant worth awakening.

Christine Carpenter

Introduction

Why This Book?

*...be admonished:
of making many books there is no end;
and much study is a weariness of the flesh.*

Ecclesiastes 12:12

Why I Wrote This Book

This is not just another book to weary the flesh, strain the eyes, and increase the spread of the posterior. However, I admit that I do not foresee the end of making books on the theme of all the women in the Bible. Why? For all of my life I have been enthralled with the Bible. My grandmother, Mama Naun, on my father's side, and my Great Aunt Lizzie on my mother's side were relentless in their Bible story telling. Both were experts and always left me wanting more.

However, it has only been in the last decade that I have discovered the women in the Bible. I am not saying that I did not know that there was an Eve with an Adam, a Sarah with an Abraham, or a Miriam with a Moses. What I am saying is that I did not know them as anything more than support actors in the stories of their men.

Unfortunately, much of the lives of Bible women went unrecorded or has been lost. In some cases what information we have is misinterpreted or even misrepresented. Too often our knowledge of Bible women is based on tradition, at best. While tradition should be considered, it should never replace what the scripture says—or does not say.

Why Read This Book

- Do you want to know the women in the Bible as well as you know the men in the Bible? If you read this book you will begin to better know the Bible women.

- Do you want to see and experience the women in the Bible as real people to whom you can relate in your own life situations? If you read this book you will begin to better know the ways of success and failure through the Bible women.

- Do you want to expand your understanding of yourself and all women? If you read this book you will begin to better know who you are by knowing more of your heritage, roots, and traditions found in the women in the Bible.

What will be the benefits of reading this book?

- You will know more of what others believe about the women in the Bible.

- You will know more of what you believe about the women in the Bible.

- You will know more of what you believe about the role of a woman today.

How to Use This Book

This book is designed to help you think through your own beliefs about the women in the Bible. In addition, it will help you sort out your own feelings and intentions toward your sisters and sisterhood as they relate to Bible women and the women in your life.

The first chapter begins with six pages of names of Bible sisters, scripture references associated with them, and a brief summary about her. Each sister can be researched further, related to your life as a role model of what to do or not do, and of course, discussed with others.

In chapters two through six the first six pages each begin with a scripture passage, followed by questions to answer. In a group, each person may be invited to read a section of scripture, a question with its possible choices, or to share an answer or thought. Committed groups may want to come prepared to discuss the material studied independently since the group last met.

If you use this book as a personal study you may want to complete one of the first six pages each day, taking the seventh day to complete the chapter. Another approach to independent study of the material in this book is to complete the first six pages on day one, followed by a new section each day. Because each section in the chapters is brief, you may want to read your way through this book a section at a time in your spare moments. Please feel free to be creative in devising a study plan that works for you or your group.

My prayer for you is that you may be enlightened, inspired, and blessed as you study these sisters and sisterhood in the Bible.

Chapter One

All the Sisters in the Bible Overview

*Every time I add another sister
to my extended family,
I find I have more room in my heart.*
                    Christine M. Carpenter

Sisters in Chronological Order

ADAH 1 & ZILLAH (Genesis 4:19, 22-23)
Both sisters were wives of Lamech; the first biblical record of polygamy; Adah bore Jabal, the ancestor of tent dwellers raising livestock, and Jubal, the ancestor of musicians of the lyre and pipe; Zillah bore Tubal-cain, maker of bronze and iron tools, and his sister Naamah.

NAAMAH 1 (Genesis 4:22)
Sister of: Tubal-Cain, founder of metal-smithing; daughter of Lamech and Zillah; half-sister to Jabal and Jubal by the same father.

MILCAH 1 (Genesis 11:29; 22:20, 23; 24:15, 24, 47)
Sister of: Lot and Ischar; niece of Abraham and Sarah; wife of Nahor, her uncle; mother of Uz, Buz, Kemuel, Chesed, Hazo, Pildash, Jidlaph, and Bethuel, the father of Rebekah.

SARI / SARAH (Genesis 17:15-21; 18:6-15; 20:2-18; 21:1-12; 23:1-19; 24:36; 25:10; 49:31; Isaiah 51:2; Romans 9:9; Galatians 11:11; 1Peter 3:6)
Sister of: Abraham, Nahor, and Haran by the same father; wife of Abraham, her half-brother; is the first Hebrew matriarch; mother of Isaac.

REBEKAH (Genesis 22:23; 24:15, 29-30, 45, 51, 53, 58-64, 67; 25:20-28; 26:8, 35; 27:5-6, 11, 15, 42, 46; 28:5; 49:31)
Sister of: Laban, the father of Jacob's wives Leah and Rachel; wife of Isaac, Sarah and Abraham's son; is the second Hebrew matriarch; mother of Esau and Jacob.

2

All the Women in the Bible: Sisters & Sisterhood

BASEMATH 2 / MAHALATH (Genesis 36:3-5; 28:9)
Sister of: Nebaioth; daughter of Ishmael, son of Abraham and Hagar; wife of Esau, son of Isaac and Rebekah; mother of Reuel.

LEAH & RACHEL (Genesis 29:6-35:23; 46:15-25; 48:7; 49:31; Ruth 4:11; Jeremiah 31:15; Matthew 2:18)
Both sisters were wives of Jacob; Leah is the third Hebrew matriarch, being Jacob's first wife, bearing him six sons (Reuben, Simeon, Levi, Judah, Issachar, and Zebulun); of the two, Rachel was Jacob's favorite, most loved wife, bearing him two sons (Joseph and Benjamin); each sister gave her maid to Jacob, and Leah's maid, Zilpah, bore Gad and Asher, and Rachel's maid, Bilhah, bore Dan and Naphtali.

DINAH (Genesis 30:21; 34:1, 3, 5, 13, 26; 46:15)
Sister of: Reuben, Simeon, Levi, Judah, Issachar, and Zebulun, the sons of Leah and Jacob; half-sister to Dan, Naphtali, Gad, Asher, Joseph, and Benjamin, all by the same father, Jacob; after her rape by Shechem, her honor was avenged by her brothers—a deed done in deception, for which their father never forgave them.

SERAH (Genesis 46:17; Numbers 26:46; 1Chronicles 7:30)
Sister of: Imnah, Ishvah, Ishvi, and Beriah; daughter of Asher, son of Jacob and Zilpah, Leah's maid.

TIMNA (Genesis 36:12, 22; 1Chronicles 1:39)
Sister of: Lotan whose father was Seir the Horite from Edom; the concubine of Eliphaz, Esau's son; mother of Amalek.

SHELOMITH 2 (1Chronicles 3:19)
Sister of: Meshullam and Hananiah; daughter of Zerubbabel, for whom the second Temple was called Zerubbabel's Temple.

All the Sisters in the Bible Overview

JOCHEBED (Exodus 6:20; Numbers 26:59)
Sister of: Gershon, Kohath, and Merari; daughter of Levi, son of Jacob and Leah; wife of Amram, her nephew; mother of Aaron, Miriam, and Moses, the deliverer of the Hebrew nation out of Egypt and through most of the wilderness experience on their way to the Promised Land.

MIRIAM (Exodus 15:20-21; Numbers 12:1, 4-5, 10, 15; 20:1; 26:59; Deuteronomy 24:9; 1Chronicles 6:3; Micah 6:4)
Sister of: Aaron and Moses; helped protect and rescue Moses from death as an infant; first Hebrew prophetess; a major leader, with her brothers, in the exodus and wilderness experience of the Hebrews.

ZIPPORAH (Exodus 2:21; 4:25; 18:2)
Sister of: six other shepherdesses, all daughters of Jethro (Reuel), the priest of Midian; wife of Moses, deliverer of the Israelites; mother and circumcisor of Gershom and Eliezer.

ELISHEBA (Exodus 6:23)
Sister of: Naashon, of the tribe of Judah; wife of Aaron, the first Levitical Hebrew priest; mother of Nadab, Abihu, Eleazar, and Ithamar.

MAHLAH & NOAH & HOGLAH & MILCAH 2 & TIRZAH (Numbers 26:33; 27:1; 36:11; Joshua 17:3)
All these sisters appeared together before the Israelite leaders in the wilderness to make their case for property inheritance rights in the Promised Land; daughters of Zelophehad, who had no sons; each married the son of their father's brothers from the clan of Manasseh; they received their father's portion of the Promised Land.

4

ACHSAH (Joshua 15:16-17; Judges 1:12- 13; 1Chronicles 2:49)
Sister of: Sheber, Tirhanah, Shaaph, and Sheva by Caleb and Maacah, Caleb's concubine; half-brothers: Jesher, Shobab, Ardon, Hur, Mesha, Mareshah, Haran, Moza, and Gazez by the same father, Caleb; after she was given to her uncle for a military prize she asked her father for a present of land, and for springs of water with it, and he gave her upper and lower springs with her gift of land.

ABIGAIL 2 & ZERUIAH (2Samuel 17:25; 1Chronicles 2:13-17) & (1Samuel 26:6; 2Samuel 2:13, 18; 3:39; 8:16; 14:1; 16:9-10; 17:25; 18:2; 19:21-22; 21:17; 23:18, 37; 1Kings 1:7; 2:5, 22; 1Chronicles 2:16; 11:6, 39; 18:12, 15; 26:28; 27:24)
Sisters of: Eliab, Abinadab, Shimea, Nethanel, Raddai, Ozem, and David; daughters of Jesse; Abigail was the mother of Amasa, by Jether the Ishmaelite; Zeruiah was the mother of Abishai, Joab, and Asahel—her name appearing twenty-five times with her sons; Zeruiah's son Joab killed Abigail's son Amasa, over military leadership.

MERAB & MICHAL (1Samuel 14:49; 18:17-20, 27-28; 19:11-13, 17; 25:44; 2Samuel 3:13-14; 6:16, 20-21, 23; 1Chronicles 15:29)
Sisters of: Jonathan, Ishvi, and Malchishua; Merab, the elder sister was promised by her father, King Saul, to be married to David, but was given to another man instead; Michael, the younger sister, loved David and became his first wife, saving him from her murderous father, but losing him to other wives and concubines.

TAMAR 2 (2Samuel 13:1-2, 4-8, 10, 19-20, 22, 32; 1Chronicles 3:9)
Sister of: Absalom by mother Maacha and father King David; half-sister by the same father, David, to: Chileab, Adonijah, Shephatiah, Ithream, Shimea, Shobab, Nathan, Solomon, Ibhar, Elishama, Eliphelet, Nogah, Nepheg, Japhia, Elishama, Eliada, Eliphelet, and Ammon, who raped her; after the rape she remained a desolate woman in the house of her brother, Absalom.

All the Sisters in the Bible Overview

TAMAR 3 (2Samuel 14:27)
Sister of: three brothers; daughter of Absalom, son of King David and Maacha; probably named for her aunt (see Tamar 2).

TAPHATH & BASEMATH 3 (1Kings 4:11) & (1Kings 4:15)
Sisters of: Rehoboam, by the same father, King Solomon; sisters of the king who succeeded his father on the throne; Taphath married Ben-abinadab, Solomon's official of all Naphath-dor; Basemath married Ahimaaz, in Naphtali; the husbands of both sisters were each responsible for providing the King's household with food one month each year.

QUEEN TAHPENES (1Kings 11:19-20)
Sister of: an unnamed woman who was given by Pharaoh of Egypt to the Edomite King Hadad; wife of Pharaoh of Egypt; after her unnamed sister gave birth to a son, Genubath, Queen Tahpenes raised him with her own sons, in her own palace in Egypt; the unnamed sister may have died in childbirth.

ATHALIAH (2Kings 8:26)
Sister of: Ahaziah, King of Israel, c. 853 B.C. for about two years and Joram, King of Israel, c. 841 B.C. for about twelve years; daughter of Ahab and Jezebel; married Jehoram, King of Judah, c. 849 B.C. for eight years; mother of Ahaziah, King of Judah, c. 847 B.C. for one year; upon son's death, took the throne by force and was the only ruling Queen of Judah, c. 835 B.C. for six years, dying violently during the political revolt that made her grandson king.

JEHOSHEBA (2Kings 11:2)
Sister of: Ahaziah by the same father, Jehoram, King of Judah, c. 849 B.C. for eight years; married to Jehoiada, the High Priest; rescued and hid her nephew, Joash, for six years from Queen Athaliah's annihilation of anyone who could challenge her place on the throne; assisted in bringing Joash to the throne c. 797 B.C. for a forty year reign.

HAZZELELPONI (1Chronicles 4:3)
Sister of: Jezreel, Ishma, and Idbash; daughter of Etam; in the genealogy of Judah around the thirteenth century B.C.

HAMMOLECHETH (1Chronicles 7:18)
Sister of: Gilead; granddaughter of Manasseh; mother of Ishod, Abiezer, and Mahalah; her Hebrew name Moleketh translates into Israelitess queen, meaning she may have been a ruler.

SHUA (1Chronicles 7:32)
Sister of: Japhlet, Shomer, and Hotham; daughter of Heber, great-grandson of Jacob and Zilpah, Leah's maid.

JEMIMAH & KEREN-HAPPUCH & KEZIAH (Job 42:14)
Sisters of: seven unnamed brothers living at the same time as the three sisters, plus seven brothers and three sisters who died before these sisters were born; daughters of Job; most beautiful women in the land; inheritors with their brothers.

MARTHA & MARY OF BETHANY (Luke 10:38-42; John 11:1-5, 19-45; 12:3)
Sisters of: Lazarus, raised to life by Jesus after four days in the tomb; Martha is known for her verbal interaction with Jesus which resulted in the resurrection of her brother and her hospitality to Jesus and his disciples; Mary is known for her spiritual attentiveness and reverent anointing of Jesus.

BERNICE & DRUSILLA (Acts 25:13, 23; 26:30-32) & (Acts 24:24)
Sisters of: Agrippa II, King of Judea from 53-100 A.D.; Bernice was wife to her uncle, Herod of Chalcis, until his death, and later wife to King Ptolemy of Sicily, for about two years, but returned to be her brother's companion; Drusilla was wife to King Aziz of Emesa, then wooed away to marry Felix; at different times both sisters heard the Apostle Paul preach.

Selected Unnamed Sisters

The Daughters of Lot
(Genesis 19:8)

The Daughters of the Midian priest
(Exodus 2:16)

The Daughters of the Judge Ibzan
(Judges 12:9)

The Daughters of Elkanah
(1Samuel 1:4)

The Daughters of Herman
(1Chronicles 25:5-6)

The Daughters of Shallum
(Nehemiah 3:12)

The Sisters of Jesus
(Matthew 13:56; Mark 6:3)

The Sister of Mary, Mother of Jesus
(John 19:25)

The Daughters of Philip
(Acts 21:9)

The Sister of Paul
(Acts 23:16)

The Sister of Nereus
(Romans 16:15)

The Elect Sister
(2John 13)

Background on Sisters

Strictly speaking, a sister can be a woman or girl who is related biologically or legally to another sibling having the same parent or parents. Also, in some situations a sister can be a very close friend. In a broader sense, a sister can be any female who is connected to the same organization, profession, race, religion, or the like.

In Bible times, daughters were expected to obey their fathers, wives their husbands, widows their male kinsmen, and sisters their brothers. There was no escaping the family and social hierarchy in Bible times, especially if you were female. In addition, younger sisters were subject to their older sisters.

Even though they were related by blood or marriage, sisters were not always friends. At times the sisters in the Bible worked together to accomplish mutual goals. At times the sisters in the Bible fought with each other. At times the sisters in the Bible fought together for each other. At times the sisters in the Bible just tolerated each other. At times the sisters in the Bible appeared to be uninvolved with one another.

An example of sisters in the Bible who worked together is found in Chapter Two where we learn about Lot's daughters. After a great deal of family upheaval, the sisters ended up living alone with their father in a cave. As he aged they saw their prospects for marriage and family dying with their father. The elder sister concocted a plan and enlisted the younger sister's help. Both sisters found unity of purpose and worked together to get their father drunk and each conceived their own son on consecutive nights. These sisters were the mothers of the men who became the fathers of the Moabites and Ammonites. Because Moab and Ammon became enemies to Israel, some scholars think that their story is a fable to mock the Moabites and Ammonites as products of incest.

We can clearly see the struggles of sisters in the Bible who fought with one another in the example in Chapter Three, which deals with the lives of Leah and Rachel. These sisters were the third generation of Hebrew matriarchs, in line after Sarah, wife of Abraham, and Rebekah, wife of Isaac, son of Sarah and Abraham. While their story appears to be one of rivalry for the love of one husband, there is a real struggle, independently, by both sisters for self-esteem. For example, according to some scholars, Rachel, being the youngest daughter and thus first in line for matrilineal descent, had a right to take from her father's house the family gods (idols—perhaps she believed they would increase her fertility). Yet others believe Rachel was trying to grasp leadership. In the end, both sisters worked together to relocate their family in the Promised Land, and Rachel's determination got her what she wanted and Leah received the honor she sought.

Mahlah, Noah, Hoglah, Milcah, and Tirzah—the daughters of Zelophehad—are the sisters of Chapter Four, and an example of sisters in the Bible who fought together for each other. These sisters worked together to petition Moses first and later Aaron for their father's portion of the Promised Land, since he had no sons to carry on his name. Working together, they were assertive in their challenge of the old ways and made a strong case for a new way. While their victory was later diminished by additional restrictions, their success is worthy of celebration. As a result of their assertive combined efforts, for the first time in recorded history, women were given the legal right to inherit property.

For an example of sisters in the Bible who tolerated each other, Chapter Five takes a new look at Martha and Mary of Bethany. Perhaps both are to be viewed in a softer light than their critics would want to promote. Through the scriptures we will see that each sister was honored for her own uniqueness and befriended and loved by Jesus for herself. While Martha displayed her friendship and Mary her reverence, both sisters were able to work together for common goals while accepting the other sister's preferred style. These sisters grew from a place of expectation and acceptance to a place of service and honor.

Finally, the example of the sisters in the Bible who appeared to be uninvolved with one another is that of the little known sisters of Chapter Six, Bernice and Drusilla. Their mutual contact in the text of the Acts of the Apostles was their presence, at different times, to hear the Apostle Paul defend himself. The presence of both sisters has been recorded in the Bible, but it was their acts recorded from hearsay that have been dramatized and have made them greater than they were in life. The lessons we have to learn from these sisters is possibly written between the lines of the actual text. While tradition paints these sisters as evil, we will look for and see Bernice's mercifulness and Drusilla's respectfulness.

Each sister has her own biblical story, and perhaps some recorded tradition or version by Cecile B. DeMill! Reading their stories with open eyes, a clear mind, and a tender heart will reveal new ways to see our biblical sisters. The same technique can be used with our earthly sisters. We all have been created in God's image and likeness. Therefore, when we take a serious look, seeking the good, we can always see some demonstration of at least one Godly Virtue.

All the Sisters in the Bible Overview

Focus Virtues

affection
assertiveness
awareness
cheerfulness
compassion
confidence
consideration
courageousness
determination
discernment
faithfulness
forgiveness
friendship
generosity
gentleness
godliness
goodness
graciousness
gratitude
harmony
holiness
honor
hopefulness
humility
joyfulness
justice

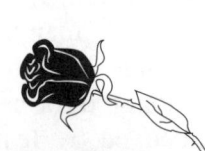

kindness
knowledge
love
loyalty
meekness
mercifulness
obedience
patience
peacefulness
purity
purposefulness
respectfulness
responsibility
reverence
righteousness
self-control
service
steadfastness
tactfulness
trust
trustworthiness
truthfulness
willingness
wisdom
understanding
unity

> A capable, intelligent and *Virtuous* woman, who . . . can find her? She is far more precious than jewels, and her value is far above rubies or pearls.
>
> **Proverbs 31:10**
> **Amplified Bible**

Why Value Virtues?

The Bible is clearly in favor of the development and exercise of Virtues. For some examples, think about the following scripture passages:

A gracious woman gets honor, but she who hates Virtue is covered with shame (Proverbs 11:16, NRSV).

According as His divine power [He] hath given unto us all things that pertain unto life and godliness, through the knowledge of Him that hath called us to glory and Virtue (2Peter 1:3, KJV).

And beside this, giving all diligence, add to your faith Virtue; and to Virtue knowledge... (2Peter 1:5, KJV).

And now, my daughter, fear not; I will do to thee all that thou requirest: for all the city of my people doth know that thou art a Virtuous woman (Ruth 3:11, KJV).

Many daughters have done Virtuously, but thou excellest them all (Proverbs 31:29, KJV).

Finally, [beloved], whatsoever things are true, whatsoever things are honest, whatsoever things are just, whatsoever things are pure, whatsoever things are lovely, whatsoever things are of good report; if there be any Virtue, and if there be any praise, think on these things (Philippians 4:8, KJV).

For the word "Virtue" some translations use "noble" or "capable". "Excellent" or "good" are also used in modern translations. In addition, "worthy" has been used along with other highly positive words which describe moral goodness. The Virtuous woman is no less than all of these—and much more.

But how did or could we become Virtuous? We were all born with the capacity for good. But how do we draw out the good—the moral excellence that is innate in all of us? For most of us, we must learn to practice moral goodness. Who taught us or should have taught us to value and practice the use of the Virtues which reside within us? The School? The Media? The Church? Our Friends? Our Parents? Our Grandparents?

And *who* will teach our children to exercise their moral responsibility—and *when*? The answers to the *who* and *when* questions are *YOU* and *NOW!* Yes, if not you, *WHO?* And if not now, *WHEN?*

But *HOW* do we teach the practice of moral responsibility?

One way to teach the practice of moral responsibility is by using the models of commonly held Virtues—moral excellence—to help build character and strengthen self-esteem in ourselves and in others, including our children.

One type of Virtues model to teach and reconfirm ourselves and others in the use of moral responsibility incorporates the stories of characters in the Bible and their use of a Focus Virtue. Each of the following chapters in this book contain one or more Focus Virtue pages. Each Focus Virtue page is intended to be inspirational as well as informative.

As we begin to understand Focus Virtues, we have

something positive to work toward instead of something negative to resist. For example, when I am angry with an inept clerk who does not know how to do her job, instead of trying *not* to be angry I begin to (re)Focus (on) Virtue. A Virtue I need to call to me during such a time could be *patience*. When I let *patience* sweep over me, my anger melts away and I know that I am walking in the spirit and not in the flesh (Romans 8:4, 5, 6, 9, 13; Galatians 5:17, 6:8; 1Peter 4:6), fulfilling the perfect law of love.

One effective way to quickly incorporate positive Virtue words and actions into our life is by using the Virtue vocabulary. The Focus Virtues are descriptors as well as names. To expedite the learning process, think of the Focus Virtues as names. Remember how powerful names have been in your past? Some I have been called are: Stupid! Clutz! Fatso! Ugly!

The "Sticks and stones may break my bones, but names will never hurt me!" song never quite neutralized the effects of the names kids called me when I was growing up. Their names stuck to me and I hear them even today. In addition, nearly everyday I hear adults negatively color me with their own impatience or prejudices. Perhaps the same is true for you, too.

Using Focus Virtues is more than an antidote which neutralizes the poisonous names we have been called, or given ourselves. Using Focus Virtues is like mainlining vitamin shots for the immune system and weight-lifting to develop and define musculature. Using Focus Virtues is as easy as naming the character quality we need or want at any given time.

We call people (and ourselves) by any number of identifiers, naming them irresponsible, mean, or depressing. Instead, why not try to call them (and ourselves) to be trustworthy, kind, or joyful. For example, when my granddaughters Krystle and Tiffany are fighting, I tell them in a peaceful tone that I need peacefulness right now—and they quiet down immediately. Then I acknowledge their peacefulness and respect for me.

For myself I need to call on wisdom when I am tempted to feel stupid; call on graciousness when I am tempted to feel like a clutz; call on self-control when I am tempted to feel fat; and call on confidence when I am tempted to feel ugly!

"The Experts" tell us that we will most likely see ourselves in the attributes others acknowledge in us. Understand that names are descriptors and descriptors are names. We will be known by the names we call ourselves. Focus Virtues make influential, powerful, successful names which build character and positive self-esteem in anyone they are bestowed upon.

William Shakespeare said, "What's in a name?" I ask you, "What's in a name?" If we truly believe that the creator's work is good, let us look for the good in others. Let us expect the good in others. Let us acknowledge the good in others—and do the same for ourselves. We were all created in the image and likeness of God, so let us look for and acknowledge God's qualities in one another. God's name is: goodness, mercifulness, patience, love.... What is true of God is true of you!

Finally, the names we are known by may be the most valuable possessions we carry throughout our life, shaping who and what we are and what we dare to do for ourselves, for others, and for God. In an early 17th Century tragedy by Shakespeare, Othello said [III. iii. 153]:

Good name in man and woman,
Dear my lord,
Is the immediate jewel of their souls;
Who steels my purse, steels trash;
'Tis something, nothing;
'Twas mine,
'Tis his and has been slave to thousands;
But he that filches from me my good name
Robs me of that which not enriches him,
And makes me poor indeed.

So, when you talk to someone, at someone, with someone, or about someone, no matter how young or how old that person is, whatever you call that person, let it be with respect, because that name could affect the rest of his or her life—and yours. Remember: Sticks and stones temporarily hurt my bones, but names forever hurt or help me. Why value Virtues? Virtues are in every person, waiting to be drawn out, seen, and demonstrated. Acknowledging Virtues in one another is one way to show that we value every person and her or his contribution to the goodness in our world.

Reflection

In the New Revised Standard Version of the Bible (NRSV), Old Testament and New Testament, the word sister appears 127 times (see next section: "Biblical Verses Containing Sister"). Sisters is used in 108 verses, but sister's in only 4. On the other hand, brother appears 278 times. Brothers is used 315, and brother's another 25 times. To sum it up, the word brother is found in 151 more scripture verses than sister. That is more than twice as many occurrences of brother than sister in the same text. Similarly, brothers makes its appearance in 207 more scriptures than does sisters. In this case, the discrepancy is nearly three to one in favor of the male term. However, brother's is the clear winner, percentage wise. With 21 more verses than its female counterpart, that turns out to be more than six times as many listings.

Many times, the word sister or sisters is not referring to females, but is used in the Bible as an analogy. For example, the words sister and sisters are used when the prophets compared cities or peoples and their wickedness or unfaithfulness toward God. The following passage is one example of the use of sister(s) in the Bible.

> *Samaria has not committed half your sins; you have committed more abominations than they, and have made your sisters appear righteous by all the abominations that you have committed. Bear your disgrace, you also, for you have brought about for your sisters a more favorable judgment; because of your sins in which you acted more abominably than they, they are more in the*

right than you. So be ashamed, you also, and bear your disgrace, for you have made your sisters appear righteous.

Ezekiel 16:51-52

In the New Revised Standard Version of the Bible, according to MacBible, at least 107 instances of the word sister(s) have been added when the word brother(s) appears. Originally, the King James Version used the word "brethren" in such instances. Strong's Exhaustive Concordance shows the Greek word brethren to be adelphos, meaning a brother (lit. or fig.) near or remote.

In short, this means that more than one hundred of the scriptures containing sister(s) are relatively new additions to the average Christian's Bible reading and hearing. This makes the ratios noted above, far greater in favor of brotherly representation for most of us who grew up on the King James Version of the Bible. During our formative years, and beyond, we have been asked to translate silently and mentally the word "brethren" to include women as well. Proponents of inclusive language acknowledge that some girls and women have been more successful than others at including themselves into the male image the writers set forth in the scriptures.

While more inclusive language has slowly evolved, it has only been recently that the New Revised Standard Version of the Bible has been widely used. Other translations have been available for sometime, with more inclusive language, however, their acceptance has not been as prevalent as the NRSV is today. With changes such as sisters and brothers instead of brethren—which means brothers—more women can hear the actual words of inclusion in more than one hundred instances.

However, the question arises as to whether or not we are rewriting the scriptures when we make such efforts for inclusion of women as sisters along with brothers—for brethren. The book of The Revelation To John gives more than a caution to anyone tampering with the content of those holy writings. Specifically, John says that *"I warn everyone who hears the words of the prophecy of this book: if anyone adds to them, God will add to that person the plagues described in this book..."* (Revelation 22:18).

If that is not a sufficient deterrent, John continues, *"...if anyone takes away from the words of the book of this prophecy, God will take away that person's share in the tree of life and in the holy city, which are described in this book"* (Revelation 22:19). This threat of being disinherited and losing one's share of the Tree of Life and the Holy City is enough for most people to leave the writings the way they are and have always been. But is there more to John's warning—or less?

First of all, it must be understood that the writings are not the way they have always been. Before and after the scriptures were translated, and sometimes retranslated, scribes rewrote the scriptures by hand for centuries. Biblical scholars agree that along the way the scribes made comments which now are accepted as the original writings. Second, John was speaking about what we commonly refer to as the book of Revelations. The Apostle Paul also wrote about the scriptures in his letter to Timothy, saying:

> *All scripture is inspired by God and is useful for teaching, for reproof, for correction, and*

for training in righteousness, so that everyone who belongs to God may be proficient, equipped for every good work.

2Timothy 3:16-17

Granted, the King James Version uses "the man of God" rather than "everyone who belongs to God". And, yes, the word man comes from anthropos and aner, meaning male, man.

However, in the context of the time it was written, women did not have access to the scriptures. In fact, it had become illegal and immoral for anyone to teach a woman the scriptures or to let a woman handle them (this is discussed in more detail later in the chapter on "Martha & Mary: The Times and Traditions"). But even that has changed. Today, women are teaching many Sunday school classes for children and adults. No one would want to stop women from touching a Bible or learning its lessons.

Most people agree that inclusive language helps women enter more fully into the Christian community and the realm of spiritual growth. Therefore, we must ask: Why would anyone want to delay or deny women this access? Why would anyone want to delay or deny anyone anything that could help fulfill a need? Delays or denials of spiritual access or spiritual development are not founded upon any biblical basis. In fact, just the opposite is true. Clearly, the Bible is in favor of teaching and learning the ways of peace with God and others. What a wonderful thing it is to not only be given the scriptural admonition to pursue spiritual principals in daily life, but also to be given the ability and assistance of the Spirit of God to attain our own spiritual goals.

Bible Verses Containing Sister

The following list notes an * to indicate scripture verses listed in the New Revised Standard Version of the Bible (NRSV) which have added the word sister(s) along with brother(s) where the word "brethren" appeared in the King James Version of the Bible. Strong's Exhaustive Concordance shows the Greek word brethren to be adelphos, meaning a brother (lit. or fig.) near or remote.

In addition, sister(s) is also used to represent nations and peoples. Sister(s) used in analogies is usually a negative connotation to a city, state, tribe, or people. Therefore it should be noted that not all scriptures which mention sister(s) are identifying a biological or legal connection between siblings.

Sister:

Gen. 4:22
Gen. 12:13
Gen. 12:19
Gen. 20:2
Gen. 20:5
Gen. 20:12
Gen. 24:30
Gen. 24:59
Gen. 24:60
Gen. 25:20
Gen. 26:7
Gen. 26:9
Gen. 28:9
Gen. 30:1
Gen. 30:8
Gen. 34:13
Gen. 34:14
Gen. 34:27
Gen. 34:31
Gen. 36:3
Gen. 36:22
Gen. 46:17
Exod. 2:4
Exod. 2:7
Exod. 6:20
Exod. 6:23
Exod. 15:20
Lev. 18:9
Lev. 18:12
Lev. 18:13
Lev. 18:18
Lev. 20:17
Lev. 20:19
Lev. 21:3
Num. 6:7
Num. 25:18
Num. 26:59
Deut. 27:22
Judg. 15:2
2Sam. 13:1
2Sam. 13:2
2Sam. 13:4
2Sam. 13:5

2Sam. 13:6
2Sam. 13:11
2Sam. 13:20
2Sam. 13:22
2Sam. 13:32
2Sam. 17:25
1Kgs. 11:19
1Kgs. 11:20
1Chr. 1:39
1Chr. 3:19
1Chr. 4:3
1Chr. 7:15
1Chr. 7:18
1Chr. 7:32
Job 17:14
Prov. 7:4
Song 4:9
Song 4:12
Song 5:2
Song 8:8
Jer. 3:7
Jer. 3:8
Jer. 3:10
Jer. 22:18
Ezek. 16:45
Ezek. 16:46
Ezek. 16:48
Ezek. 16:49
Ezek. 16:56
Ezek. 22:11
Ezek. 23:4
Ezek. 23:11
Ezek. 23:18
Ezek. 23:31
Ezek. 23:33
Ezek. 44:25
Hosea 2:1
*Matt. 5:22
*Matt. 5:23
*Matt. 5:24
Matt. 12:50
*Matt. 18:35
Mark 3:35
Luke 10:39
Luke 10:40
John 11:1
John 11:5
John 11:28
John 11:39
John 19:25
*Acts 23:16
*Rom. 14:10
*Rom. 14:15
*Rom. 14:21
Rom. 16:1
Rom. 16:15
*1Cor. 5:11
1Cor. 7:15
*1Ths. 4:6
*Phlm. 2
James 2:15
*1Pet. 5:13
*1John 2:9
*1John 2:10
*1John 3:15
*1John 3:17
*1John 4:20
*1John 5:16
2John 13

Sisters:

Gen. 24:30
Gen. 29:13
Lev. 20:17
Josh. 2:13
1Chr. 2:16
Job 1:4
Job 42:11
*Ps. 22:22
Ezek. 16:45
Ezek. 16:51
Ezek. 16:52
Ezek. 16:55
Ezek. 16:61
Ezek. 23:32
*Matt. 5:47
Matt. 13:56
Matt. 19:29
*Mark 3:32
Mark 6:3
Mark 10:29
Mark 10:30

Luke 14:26	*1Cor. 16:15	*2Ths. 2:1
John 11:3	*1Cor. 16:20	*2Ths. 2:13
*Acts 16:40	*2Cor. 1:8	*2Ths. 2:15
*Rom. 1:13	*2Cor. 8:1	*2Ths. 3:1
*Rom. 7:1	*2Cor. 11:26	*2Ths. 3:13
*Rom. 8:12	*2Cor. 13:11	*1Tim. 4:6
*Rom. 10:1	*Gal. 1:11	1Tim. 5:2
*Rom. 11:25	*Gal. 3:15	*2Tim. 4:21
*Rom. 12:1	*Gal. 5:13	*Hebr. 2:11
*Rom. 15:14	*Gal. 6:18	*Hebr. 2:12
*Rom. 15:30	*Phil. 1:14	*Hebr. 2:17
*Rom. 16:14	*Phil. 3:1	*Hebr. 3:1
*Rom. 16:17	*Phil. 3:17	*Hebr. 3:12
*1Cor. 1:10	*Phil. 4:1	*Hebr. 13:22
*1Cor. 1:11	*Col. 1:2	*James 1:2
*1Cor. 1:26	*Col. 4:15	*James 2:1
*1Cor. 2:1	*1Ths. 1:4	*James 2:5
*1Cor. 3:1	*1Ths. 2:1	*James 2:14
*1Cor. 4:6	*1Ths. 2:9	*James 3:1
*1Cor. 7:24	*1Ths. 2:14	*James 3:10
*1Cor. 7:29	*1Ths. 2:17	*James 3:12
*1Cor. 10:1	*1Ths. 3:7	*James 4:11
*1Cor. 11:33	*1Ths. 4:1	*James 5:19
*1Cor. 12:1	*1Ths. 4:9	*1Pet. 5:9
*1Cor. 14:6	*1Ths. 4:10	*2Pet. 1:10
*1Cor. 14:20	*1Ths. 4:13	*1John 3:10
*1Cor. 15:1	*1Ths. 5:1	*1John 3:13
*1Cor. 15:6	*1Ths. 5:12	*1John 4:20
*1Cor. 15:31	*1Ths. 5:26	*1John 4:21
*1Cor. 15:50	*2Ths. 1:3	*Rev. 6:11

Virtues Reflection: Overview

The sisters in the Old Testament and New Testament are included in the scriptures for a variety of reasons—some reasons are clearer than others. We will consider three reasons. *First, there are sisters who displayed developed Virtues to be admired and emulated. Second, there are sisters who displayed the need to exercise their developed Virtues. Third, there are sisters who displayed the need for further development of the Virtues they had.*

As we read, ponder, and discuss the stories of the sisters in the Bible, we can begin our own list of Bible based womanly Virtues. For example, look at Miriam, the sister of Moses and Aaron. As you read her story in the scriptures, what are the Virtues you identify in her? *Obedience? Reverence? Creativity? Trust?* Take a few moments to identify her developed Virtues, then complete the following exercise with Miriam in mind. (You can use this technique to read about other Bible sisters and answer these questions.)

Which one of the developed Virtues of this Bible sister do you most appreciate, today? Why this Virtue?

What do you admire most about this Bible sister and/or her Focus Virtue?

How has this Focus Virtue been part of your life in the past or in the present?

How do you see this Focus Virtue or the need for it in your life, now?

What can you do to further develop this Focus Virtue in your life?

What has helped you most as a result of this study?

Action Scripture

1John 3:17-19 *How does God's love abide in anyone who has the world's goods and sees a brother or sister in need and yet refuses help? Little children, let us love, not in word or speech, but in truth and action. And by this we will know that we are from the truth and will reassure our hearts before him.*

Grateful Prayer

LORD God, You have made us sisters and brothers. Guide us in all we do and bring us into greater appreciation of all our sisters and brothers. Open our eyes to see and be inspired by the sisters in the Bible. Help us learn from one another so that we may find the meaning and rewards of sisterhood and brotherhood. Strengthen our relationships with one another and lead us to those who need and want to share in our sisterhood and brotherhood. AMEN

Chapter Two

Lot's Daughters

*It is impossible to see sisterhood
if you do not look for it.*
                    Christine M. Carpenter

Lot's Daughters

> **Excerpts from Gen. 19:1-8** The two angels came to Sodom in the evening...When Lot saw them, he rose to meet them, and bowed down with his face to the ground. He said, "Please, my lords, turn aside to your servant's house and spend the night...But before they lay down, the men of the city, the men of Sodom, both young and old, all the people to the last man, surrounded the house; and they called to Lot, "Where are the men who came to you tonight? Bring them out to us, so that we may know them." Lot went out of the door to the men, shut the door after him, and said, "I beg you, my brothers, do not act so wickedly. Look, I have two daughters who have not known a man; let me bring them out to you, and do to them as you please; only do nothing to these men, for they have come under the shelter of my roof." . . .

While their father made his proposal to the men of the town, what do you think the sisters were:

a. Feeling?   b. Thinking?

c. Saying?   d. Doing?

e. Planning?   f. Hoping?

g. Expecting?   h. Other?

For a moment, put yourself in the position of Lot's daughters, and imagine if your father made such a proposal to anyone, what would you be:

a. Feeling?   b. Thinking?

c. Saying?   d. Doing?

e. Planning?   f. Hoping?

g. Expecting?   h. Other?

> **Excerpts from Gen. 19:9-14** But they replied, "Stand back...This fellow came here as an alien, and he would play the judge! Now we will deal worse with you than with them." Then they pressed hard against the man Lot, and came near the door to break it down. But the men inside reached out their hands and brought Lot into the house...And they struck with blindness the men who were at the door of the house...so that they were unable to find the door. Then the men said to Lot, "Have you anyone else here?...bring them out of the place. For we are about to destroy this place, because the outcry against its people has become great before the LORD...So Lot went out and said to his sons-in-law, who were to marry his daughters, "Up, get out of this place; for the LORD is about to destroy the city." But he seemed to his sons-in-law to be jesting.

What was the crowd trying to do to Lot and why?

Where were Lot's sons-in-law when "both young and old, all the people to the last man," surrounded the house of Lot?

a. They had been in the crowd with the other men of the city.
b. They were at home with their mother because they were still too young to go out at night without adult supervision (they had been betrothed to Lot's daughters from birth).
c. They were traveling home from a business trip to Zoar when the crowd was at Lot's house.
d. Other?

Why did the Angels include Lot's sons-in-law in the escape plan?

What would make Lot's sons-in-law think that Lot was jesting about the LORD destroying the city?

Lot's Daughters

> **Gen. 19:15-17** When morning dawned, the angels urged Lot, saying, "Get up, take your wife and your two daughters who are here, or else you will be consumed in the punishment of the city." But he lingered; so the men seized him and his wife and his two daughters by the hand, the LORD being merciful to him, and they brought him out and left him outside the city. When they had brought them outside, they said, "Flee for your life; do not look back or stop anywhere in the Plain; flee to the hills, or else you will be consumed."

Why did Lot remain until morning, after he was told to take his family out of the city the night before?

a. He was waiting for his sons-in-law to take him seriously and join the family in their departure.

b. He did not realize that the destruction was going to happen so soon.

c. He was trying to figure out how he could get all his possessions out of town.

d. He was hoping it was not true and he could stay in his home.

e. Other?

What were the sisters, Lot's daughters, doing all night?

a. Packing.   b. Praying.

c. Sleeping.   d. Crying.

e. Worrying.   f. Other?

What would you have been doing that night if you were one of these sisters?

> **Excerpts from Gen. 19:18-26** And Lot said to them, "Oh, no, my lords; your servant has found favor with you, and you have shown me great kindness in saving my life; but I cannot flee to the hills, for fear the disaster will overtake me and I die. Look, that city is near enough to flee to, and it is a little one. Let me escape there—is it not a little one?—and my life will be saved!" He said to him, "Very well, I grant you this favor too, and will not overthrow the city of which you have spoken. Hurry, escape there, for I can do nothing until you arrive there."...Then the LORD rained on Sodom and Gomorrah sulfur and fire from the LORD out of heaven; and he overthrew those cities, and all the Plain, and all the inhabitants of the cities, and what grew on the ground. But Lot's wife, behind him, looked back, and she became a pillar of salt.

Why did the mother of the sisters look back?

a. She turned around to tell the girls to hurry.
b. She saw a light in back of her that was brighter than anything she had ever seen before and wanted a closer look.
c. She wanted to see how close the disaster was getting to her family and keep them ahead of it.
d. She fell down and getting up her eyes turned toward the light.
e. Other?

Why didn't the sisters look back?

a. They were obedient young girls.
b. They were behind their mother and saw what happened to her.
c. They did, but God knew they were just kids and helped them.
d. They were too busy running away from the noise, smell, and light.
e. Other?

Lot's Daughters

> **Gen. 19:30-33** Now Lot went up out of Zoar and settled in the hills with his two daughters, for he was afraid to stay in Zoar; so he lived in a cave with his two daughters. And the firstborn said to the younger, "Our father is old, and there is not a man on earth to come in to us after the manner of all the world. Come, let us make our father drink wine, and we will lie with him, so that we may preserve offspring through our father." So they made their father drink wine that night; and the firstborn went in, and lay with her father; he did not know when she lay down or when she rose.

If you were one of these sisters, what would you have done to survive after Sodom?

a. Gone back home to Sodom and looked for my fiancée.
b. Looked in Zoar and neighboring towns for another man to marry.
c. Found domestic work and pooled my finances with my sister and father.
d. Sold myself as a slave and given the money to my sister and father.
e. Other?

What do you think were all the reasons the elder sister devised her plan to lay with her father and then suggested that her younger sister do the same?

Why did the older sister share her plan with her younger sister?

a. She was hoping she would talk her out of it.
b. She was hoping her sister had a better plan.
c. She really needed help getting him drunk.
d. She told her sister everything.
e. Other?

> **Gen. 19:34-38** On the next day, the firstborn said to the younger, "Look, I lay last night with my father; let us make him drink wine tonight also; then you go in and lie with him, so that we may preserve offspring through our father." So they made their father drink wine that night also; and the younger rose, and lay with him; and he did not know when she lay down or when she rose. Thus both the daughters of Lot became pregnant by their father. The firstborn bore a son, and named him Moab; he is the ancestor of the Moabites to this day. The younger also bore a son and named him Ben-ammi; he is the ancestor of the Ammonites to this day.

Why did the younger sister go along with the plan of her older sister?

a. She was always obedient in everything her elders suggested, requested, or required of her.

b. She thought it sounded like fun to trick her father, twice.

c. She was afraid to question her elder sister about anything she said to do.

d. She could not think of a better plan and knew they needed at least one man in the house.

e. Other?

What kind of relationship do you think the sisters had before, during, and after having sons?

What kind of relationships do you have with your biological and/or spiritual sisters?

As a result of this lesson, what will you take into consideration before you judge the behaviors of your sister(s)?

Lot's Daughters

Lot's Daughters' Family Tree

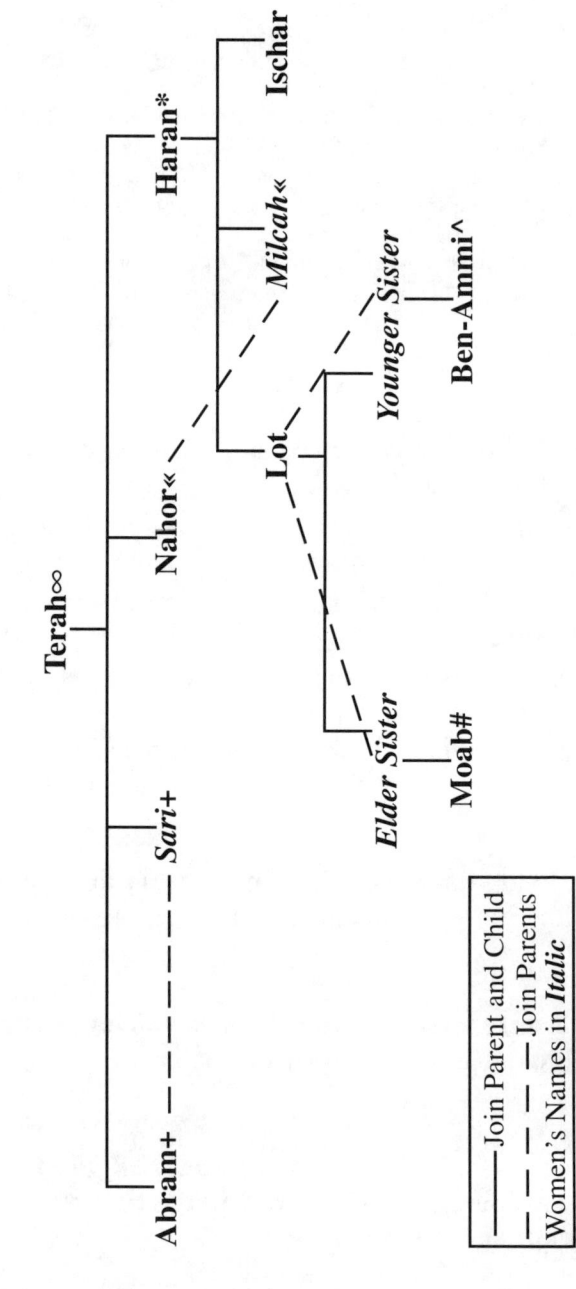

Terah∞
├── Abram+ ------ *Sari*+
└── Nahor«
└── Haran*
    ├── Ischar
    ├── *Milcah*«
    └── Lot
        ├── *Elder Sister* — Moab#
        └── *Younger Sister* — Ben-Ammi^

───── Join Parent and Child
– – – Join Parents
Women's Names in *Italic*

*For a more detailed Family Tree, see Chapter Three: Leah & Rachel's Family Tree

∞Grandfather of Lot; Gen. 11:27 Now these are the descendants of Terah. Terah was the father of Abram, Nahor, and Haran; and Haran was the father of Lot.

*Haran, Lot's father, died before Terah, Lot's grandfather; Gen. 11:28 Haran died before his father Terah in the land of his birth, in Ur of the Chaldeans. [Comment: perhaps, on the death of their brother, Haran, Nahor assumed responsibility for his niece, Milcah, and Abram assumed responsibility for his nephew, Lot.]

+Sarai was Abram's half-sister and wife; Gen. 11:29 Abram and Nahor took wives; the name of Abram's wife was Sarai, and the name of Nahor's wife was Milcah. She was the daughter of Haran the father of Milcah and Iscah.; Gen. 20:11 Abraham said, "I did it because I thought, There is no fear of God at all in this place, and they will kill me because of my wife. Gen. 20:12 Besides, she is indeed my sister, the daughter of my father but not the daughter of my mother; and she became my wife. Gen. 20:13 And when God caused me to wander from my father's house, I said to her, 'This is the kindness you must do me: at every place to which we come, say of me, He is my brother.'"

«Milcah was Nahor's niece and wife; Gen. 11:29 Abram and Nahor took wives; the name of Abram's wife was Sarai, and the name of Nahor's wife was Milcah. She was the daughter of Haran the father of Milcah and Iscah.

#Moab (meaning from her [the mother's] father) is the father of the Moabites; Gen. 19:36-37 Thus both the daughters of Lot became pregnant by their father. The firstborn bore a son, and named him Moab; he is the ancestor of the Moabites to this day. (Note: NRSV lists Moab 170 times, Moabites, 19, and Moabite 12.)

^Ben-Ammi (meaning son of my people) is the father of the Ammonites; Gen. 19:38 The younger also bore a son and named him Ben-ammi; he is the ancestor of the Ammonites to this day. (Note: NRSV lists Ammon 9, Ammonites 115 times, Ammonite, 16.)

35

Sodom & Gomorrah Facts & Theories:

Time & Location of Sodom & Gomorrah

The historical Sodom and Gomorrah recorded in the Bible is believed to have existed during the Early Bronze Age. This is when Abraham and Lot are thought to have lived in or around the area. For the stories of Abraham and Lot, the biblical time was around 1900 B.C.

Gene Faulstich, founder of the Chronology-History Research Institute and a specialist in astronomical-based historical chronology has combined secular chronology and astronomical data with the use of computers to pinpoint specific dates in biblical history. Using these tools, Faulstich explored the idea that an earthquake was part of the events of the destruction of Sodom and Gomorrah. Since earthquakes are more likely to occur during the extra gravitational pull of an eclipse, and a double rising and setting of the sun is recorded in the biblical text, his computer says the destruction took place Friday, October 29, 1952 B.C.

As for the location, the area where it is believe that Sodom and Gomorrah were located is now what we refer to as the Dead Sea. In the King James Version the Bible calls it the salt sea (Genesis 14:3), the sea of the plain (Deuteronomy 3:17), the east sea (Joel 2:20), and the former sea (Zechariah 14:8). Located southeast of Jerusalem, the Dead Sea is an inland body of salt water between Israel and Jordan. It covers about 370 square miles and is approximately 1,290 feet below sea level. The Dead Sea is the lowest known surface of the earth.

Dr. William H. Shea, a research associate with the Biblical Research Institute in Washington, D.C., and author of more than one hundred articles on Near Eastern archaeology, cites evidence to the actual existence of Sodom and Gomorrah. This particular archaeological finding is a tablet diary of cities visited by a merchant from Elba during the Early Bronze Age, just before Abraham and Lot's time in the area. The 4,500-year-old tablet is called the *Eblaite Geographic Atlas.* Shea says that:

> It contains a list of 290 place names. I have studied about 80 of these place names in two different segments. These two segments of the list give names that run through the land of Canaan, where the ancient biblical patriarchs lived. The second segment cuts from the central hill country of Canaan east towards the Dead Sea, around the south end of the Dead Sea, and then up to the plateau of Jordan, and finally south to the Gulf of Aqabah. Of particular interest is name number 210, Admah in the old Canaanite form. That's Admah from the biblical list of the cities of the plain from Genesis 14. The next name, number 211, is very interesting because it is written with signs that are unmistakably clear...Sadam, or Sodom, the biblical Sodom....It's the final name on the list of this merchant's travels. Aqabah is obviously the Gulf of Aqabah, and that confirms that he had traveled through Sadam south of the Dead Sea. That's where the biblical Sodom was located.

Dr. Marvin A. Luckerman, publisher of the *Catastrophes of Ancient History Journal*, and Middle East scholar, with a M.A. in Islamic Studies from the University of California at Los Angeles says that:

> ...Sodom and Gomorrah were located on a fault that runs from Turkey to Central Africa, and that this fault was very active seismically. Also in the same area was pitch and oil that even today bubbles up to the surface of the water....the earthquakes, the petroleum in the area, creates the possibility for a disaster that would have destroyed all five cities of the plain.

When Lot fled Sodom he asked to go to Zoar. The location of Zoar has been confirmed from the Madaba Map, a mosaic on the floor of a Madaba, Jordan church. The mosaic dates from the fifth century A.D., showing Jerusalem in the center, Jericho, Zoar just at the southern end of the Dead Sea, as well as the Jordan River flowing into the Dead Sea.

Geology of Sodom and Gomorrah

Today the mountain of Sodom is a piece of salt approximately eight miles long. "But what can be seen is only the tip of the iceberg," says Shlomo Goren, director of information for the Dead Sea Industries. Further, Goren says that the mountain is two miles deep, almost entirely composed of salt. He points out that strange layers and caves can be seen, which were "created by the penetration of water, which suggests an outlet to the top." This erosion lends itself to strange shapes, one of which has been identified as "Lot's wife."

It is believed that this area was formerly fertile, which is why Lot selected it when he separated from Abraham (Genesis 13:10). In time, it is believed that seismic activity and the explosion of subterranean gases changed the face of the area. Geologists believe that there is a great stratum of rock salt lying under the Mountain of Sodom on the west shore of the Dead Sea. The stratum of salt, has a layer of stratum of marl, mingled with very pure free sulphur.

Genesis 14:10 says that the Valley of Siddim (the Dead Sea) was full of bitumen (asphalt) pits. On the day Lot and his family were forced by the angels to flee the city (Genesis 19:24), it is believed that something kindled the gasses that accumulated with the oil and asphalt, producing an explosion. It is conjectured that red hot salt and sulphur blew into the sky and actually rained down fire and brimstone on the area of Sodom and Gomorrah! This is a favored explanation for the utter destruction of the cities, the plain, and everything that once grew out of the ground in what had been a fertile, agriculturally productive area.

Dr. Revell Phillips, Professor of Geology, says that it is possible that Lot's wife may have been overcome by poison gasses, ash, and volcanic activity shaking and quaking the ground she tried to walk on. If she fell in the shallow water of the Dead Sea, the most saline body of water on the Earth, in a short period of time she would become encrusted with salt. Dr. Phillips notes the geologic conditions of the area, including the possibility of volcanic activity:

> The earth's crust is divided into a number of rigid plates that interact with each other in

three ways...The Middle East is an active area in which the plates are spreading apart in a V kind of action.

The Rift Valley, which extends from Syria down through the Sea of Galilee, the Jordan Valley, the Dead Sea, and ultimately into the Gulf of Aqaba and the Red Sea, is a spreading center. As the plates spread apart, a block of rock called the Graben Valley drops between the two plates. This is the Jordan Valley, the Dead Sea region. As the plates jostle and separate, there is considerable earthquake activity. The destruction of Sodom and Gomorrah, located at the southern tip of the Dead Sea, fits the description of typical earthquake and volcanic activity combined.

Also concurring, that the destruction of Sodom and Gomorrah may well have been a volcanic eruption, is Dr. Philip Hammond, a Middle East Field Archaeologist. As evidence to his volcanic eruption theory, he sights the presence of poisonous gasses, sulfur, salt, asphalt, and tar.

Frederick Clapp, a geologist, investigated the whole region and though he was unable to verify volcanic activity, he found evidence of deposits of petroleum products around the southern end of the Dead Sea. Clapp proposes the theory that the Rift Valley settled down, causing that movement or earthquake to put pressure on the petroleum deposits, gas, oil, and bitumen—which is basically asphalt—forcing them to come up through the existing fault line and into the air. All it would have taken was a spark or a fire to ignite the gasses into flaming materials which would then fall back down upon the cities and plain, destroying them.

In addition, Professor Randall Younker, Director of the Horn Archaeological Museum points out that three out of five sites along the Dead Sea have shown to have an ash layer when they were excavated. The ash layer indicates that they were terminated by fire, quite abruptly, near the end of the Bronze Age.

Life in Sodom and Gomorrah

Dr. Steven Collins, professor of cultural anthropology specializes in ancient climates and believes that Sodom and Gomorrah would have had a climate during the time of Abraham and Lot which would have supported grasslands enough to provide for a wide range of domesticated animals and a wild animal population similar to North Africa. By 1000 B.C., however, because of deforestation to construct buildings and provide for other domestic, cultural, and survival needs, the climate changed dramatically. But while Abraham and Lot built their flocks, the area was well able to support them, and in fact, according to Collins, they were able to "make a grand living in this part of the world."

A reporter for the Jordan Times, Rami G. Khouri, reported that:

> They [Dr. Walter Rast and Dr. R. Thomas Schaub] discovered that Bab edh-Dhra [Sodom] was not an isolated urban phenomenon in an otherwise sparsely populated area. Rather, it was the largest and northernmost of a line of Early Bronze Age

town sites along the southeast shore of the Dead Sea, that were also adjacent to fertile agricultural lands and had good sources of fresh water nearby....

Khouri also commented on the findings pertaining to agriculture during Abraham and Lot's time in the area.

Flotation of plant remains from Bab edh-Dhra indicates the people were growing and harvesting wheat, barley, grapes, olives, figs, lentils, chickpeas, flax, pistachio, almond and assorted wild plants, with strong evidence that irrigated agriculture was practiced....

Continuing to comment on the animal population of the locale around Sodom and Gomorrah during the approximate time Abraham and Lot inhabited the area, Khouri writes:

Bone remains show that animal species that existed at Bab edh-Dhra, whether to be eaten, used as beasts of burden or for other reasons, included sheep and goats, donkeys, camels, gazelles, cats, dogs, hyenas, rodents, lizards or turtles, and possibly some fish and birds.

Dr. Bryant G. Wood, a Syro-Palestinian archaeologist also agrees that the region was lush in Abraham and Lot's time. His evidence comes from excavation of very large cemeteries in the area of Sodom and Gomorrah. There, he and other archaeologists, found tens of thousands of people buried, at least 50,000.

By studying the skeletal remains, anthropologists determined that the people of the area were "very, very prosperous," according to Wood. He noted that the people appeared to be healthy, which means that they were partakers of a good diet. The basis for his evaluation comes partly from the observation of the stature of the people found buried in the cemeteries. While the average height for people of the time was about five feet, two inches, these folk were quite a bit taller, some being over six feet tall.

Finally, human life-style is also evident by what remains in the area from the time of Abraham and Lot. For example, Wood reports that excavations of Sodom (Bab edh-Dhra) and four other cities in the area of the plains leads anthropologists to believe that the life-style of the people of that time, in those places, was not what we would call a normal *family* life. His assumption is based on the examination of cemeteries. The burial sites are said to have been of a communal type of life. No family groupings among the 50,000 bodies have been discovered in the burial sites, according to Professor Randall Younker, director of the Horn Archaeological Museum, Amman, Jordan.

Why Save Lot & His Family?

Summary of Genesis 18: The LORD appeared to Abraham by the oaks of Mamre, along with two angels, all taking the form of men. Abraham ran to meet them, and bowed down to the ground, asking them to stop and take a meal with him. Afterward, the men set out toward Sodom and Abraham went with them to point the way. Before they departed, the LORD told Abraham what He was about to do to Sodom and Gomorrah because of the severity of their sin! Then the two men (angels) went toward Sodom, while Abraham remained standing before the LORD. Abraham began to negotiate with the LORD, reminding Him that He was a just Judge and would not let the righteous be killed with the unrighteous in the city. Abraham asked that the city not be destroyed if there were fifty righteous in the city. The LORD said that if that were the case, He would forgive the whole city for the sake of the fifty righteous who lived there. Humbly, Abraham asked the LORD if there were only forty-five righteous in the city would He spare the city? The LORD agreed. Again Abraham asked if there were only forty, and the LORD said the whole city would be spared for the sake of the forty righteous living there. Abraham asked that the LORD not be angry with him for asking in the case of thirty, and the LORD said He would spare it for thirty. Abraham asked if twenty were found that the LORD not destroy it and the LORD agreed for twenty. Abraham asked to speak just once more, in the case of only ten righteous. The LORD answered that He would not destroy the city if ten righteous were found in it. Then the LORD went on His way and Abraham returned to his place.

The Mother of Lot's Daughters

When pondering the biblical record of the life and the death of Lot's wife, the mother of Lot's two daughters, it might be interesting to consider the following questions:

- What do we know from the scriptures about the character of Lot's wife?
- Why is there no mention in the scriptures of Lot's wife's prodding or intervention in his dealings with others—or at all?
- Why was Lot ahead of his wife when they fled and not next to her, helping her flee the destruction?
- Why did Lot's wife turn to salt: Geologically? Physically? Mentally? Spiritually?
- In what context is he speaking and what point is he making when Jesus says, *"Remember Lot's wife"* (Luke 17:32)?
- Does tradition read more or less into the story and character of Lot's wife?

Lot's wife is often thought to be a woman who ate, drank, and cared more for the things of the world than for spiritual things. Where did Lot's wife get such a bad reputation? The answer is not from the reading of the Genesis scriptures, but from the reading of modern and ancient writers. For example, in *Wives of the Bible*, by Dr. William B. Riley, asserts that:

> When we have read Lot's history we have uncovered Mrs. Lot's character; and when we have studied his affluence...The character and conduct of children reflect the mother. The marriage of her daughters to Sodomitish

men indicated low ethical ideals and low moral standards.

While these comments make for interesting reading by some, they do not reflect the tradition of the times in which the people in Genesis lived. In their day, men were in charge and women held their place just below livestock. We note how easily Lot gave his virgin daughters to a crowd of rapists rather than have strangers harmed. It is difficult to believe that Mrs. Lot, as she is referred to by Riley, sent Lot out to make the offer or was in agreement with her husband's decision to turn over the girls to the mob.

Nor is it reasonable to believe that Mrs. Lot arranged the marriages of her daughters to the men of Sodom. During those times fathers had total control of marriage arrangements, not mothers, as we will see in the next chapter when we look at the marriage arrangements of Leah and Rachel. Blaming Mrs. Lot has gotten Lot off the hook for centuries. However, the low moral and ethical standards displayed by Lot are not likely to have been the direct result of his wife's ability to change his character, any more than a wife of today is able to change the character of her husband—though she may try!

Also contributing to further create a negative reputation for Lot's wife and her daughters, is Ruben's painting entitled the "Flight of Lot." His 1625 painting, which now hangs in the Louvre, shows Lot's daughters as they flee Sodom bearing gold and silver, along with baskets loaded with fruit. In the painting Lot's wife, has her hands clasped, looking sullen as she stares into the face of the angel who is warning her to flee in order to save her from destruction. The colorful, vivid picture is a work of art by an artist who is creating a feeling for the moment. It is not a snapshot in time of the actual events—events which are sometimes disputed and even discounted as fictional.

The poem, "Lot's Wife", by Max Eastman promotes the idea that Lot's wife was ungodly, saying, "Herself, like Sodom's towers, shone blazingly." Poetic license is necessary for crafting literature, but too often the written word becomes gospel—carrying as much weight or more weight than scripture. Such is the case with "Lot's Wife."

In *Ancient Secrets of the Bible,* authors Charles E. Sellier and Brian Russell add their dramatization to the Lot story when they put the following words into the mouths of the characters:

> "Why did Mother stay behind?" the other daughter asked. "She was with us for miles, and suddenly I did not hear her complaining voice anymore. And you would not let us look back."
> Lot stroked his beard in obvious grief.
> "Let's leave her to the mercies of a righteous God. I, too, miss her already, despite her complaints at our sudden departure from the home we loved so much...."

Traditionally, Lot's wife has been blamed for his choice of the fertile plain of the Jordan, leaving his Uncle Abraham with the lesser of the choice land. Also, she is voiced to be the culprit who brought the family to Sodom to satisfy her selfishness, greed, and materialism. For example, In her book, *All of the Women of the Bible,* Edith Deen says, "Though we have no record of his wife in this transaction, we again can visualize her as a woman sharing in his

Lot's Daughters

selfishness, without dissent, and prodding her husband to greater wealth at any cost to others." In addition, Deen says that, "Lot's wife was a native of this area and her evil influence carried on into the daughters."

Deen is to be commended on her accuracy in acknowledging that we have no record of Lot's wife in the transaction between Lot and Abraham for the fertile plain of the Jordan (see Genesis 13:10-11). To go farther, it should be acknowledged that we have no record of the origin of Lot's wife, whether she was an evil influence, or selfishly prodded her husband. It is only through the visualizations of Deen, and others, that we are able to see the wickedness of Lot's wife and daughters.

In fact, the following are all the Bible references referring to Lot's wife:

> **Genesis 19:15-16** *But when morning dawned, the angels urged Lot, saying, "Get up, take your **wife** and your two daughters who are here, or else you will be consumed in the punishment of the city." But he lingered; so the men seized him and his **wife** and his two daughters by the hand, the LORD being merciful to him, and they brought him out and left him outside the city.*
> **Genesis 19:26** *But Lot's **wife**, behind him, looked back, and she became a pillar of salt.*
> **Luke 17:32** *Remember Lot's **wife**.*

When we look into scripture, we hear the angels speaking, repeatedly to Lot, telling him to take his wife and daughters to safety. We may want to ask ourselves why Lot delayed? And why did he go on ahead of his wife and daughters, instead of remaining beside them to help them escape the destruction?

If we think of the angel's warning, in context of what we know today, perhaps the angel's warning was just that—a warning. Where would be the condemnation of Lot's wife if the angel was giving a warning that if anyone paused even for a moment, in this case for just a quick look, that moment of delay would be enough to get caught in the upheaval of geological forces that were destroying Sodom and Gomorrah? The onlooker would also be destroyed—not because of any sodomish sin, but because of the delay of pausing and looking. Perhaps she did not pause of her own accord, but was shaken to the ground and unable to recover herself. She may even have demanded that the others leave her and save themselves. We do not know what happened.

Perhaps the concept of Lot's wife as a worldly, rather than a spiritually, focused woman may come from the misinterpretation of Luke 17:32. In the Luke scripture, Jesus said, *"Remember Lot's wife."* This second shortest verse in the Bible is in context with the story of Sodom and why it was destroyed—as was Lot's wife—and how a similar destruction was coming upon the earth because of sin. What did Jesus mean when he said to remember Lot's wife? —If you delay you will not be saved. It is a fact that the rain (end) comes, for the just and the unjust, all the same!

In short, tradition has made much more of Lot's wife than the scriptures and sound biblical scholarship can support. She is not entitled to all the negative attributes which have been bestowed upon her. However, she has served to shift the blame from Lot as head of his household, or to excuse Lot's behavior in any and all questionable situations. By projecting the blame on Lot's wife, his daughters have been incriminated and Lot exonerated.

Reflection

Genesis gives us a picture of two sisters who were betrothed to be married. Their betrothed did not believe Lot's warning to flee the destruction to come. We have no record of why they would think Lot was joking. Perhaps they were just boys or young men, betrothed to Lot's daughters when all of them were babies. The scriptures say that Lot's daughters were girls, therefore their betrothed may have been boys, accustomed to Lot joking with them. The sons-in-law are never referred to as men, and there is no indication that they were present in the crowd that was blinded, as described in Geneses 19, being comprised of "men of Sodom, both young and old, all the people to the last man". However old they were, they thought Lot was joking, and so died in the destruction of Sodom.

However, their betrothed wives, Lot's daughters, were forced by the angels to flee the city without their intended mates. Lot's daughters, for whatever reasons—obedience to the angels warning or a devout focus on going forward, or the favor of God—did not befall the same fate as their mother. However, while their life was spared, they lost their intended husbands, mother, friends, other relatives, house, clothes, trousseau, hope chest, personal mementos, places of childhood memories, future dreams, social status, security, and sustaining.

What they had now was each other and a father. They also had the memory of their father giving them to the crowd to do whatever sexual exploit the crowd desired, instead of their father protecting them from the crowd and preserving their virginity for their marriage—as was the requirement of the time. In addition, they had the memory of Lot fleeing in front of his wife, and not being by her side to help her physically and spiritually. Also, they had the memory of a fearful father: fearful that the crowd in Sodom would mistreat his guests who were under his protection, as was the custom of the day, because they had eaten in his home (Genesis 19:6-8); fearful of not being able to do as the angels said and flee into the hills in time to avoid the destruction of Sodom, and instead asking to go to a nearby town (Genesis 19:19-20); and fearful to live among the people of Zoar and taking his daughters to live in a cave (Genesis 19:30).

Lot's daughters lived with him in a cave. When Lot was old, and his daughters had no prospects of marriage or offspring, the older daughter discussed and led the plan for the daughters each to have a child by their father. The scriptural picture shows two sisters working together in unity to secure their desired results—sons. It is more than likely that the two sisters had developed their unity over time and through the challenges of living a secluded life in a cave with an aging father. Now they were uniting to not just sustain life but to perpetuate life.

Lot's daughters, by today's standards, were guilty of incest with their father. However, the Bible does not condemn their behavior in its retelling. It is not until Leviticus 18, long after these Genesis characters, that we have record of such an act being incestuous. Remember, Abraham and Sarah were half-brother and sister by the same father, as well as husband and wife; Nahor and Milcah were uncle and niece, as well as husband and wife; both Abraham and Nahor were great uncles to Lot's daughters. By the same standards of incest in Leviticus, both Abraham and Nahor were as guilty of incest as Lot's daughters.

We do not know if extraordinary sexual relations with close relatives was taboo in their day. Certainly, there is no record that God condemned the sisters for having sexual relations with their father or punished them in any way. In fact, both offspring became great nations. We do know, however, that the biological mandate to reproduce—continuation of the species—was a major theme in scripture and other recorded histories. These sisters had more than their biological clocks ticking; the responsibility to perpetuate their father's name was also an issue. We will see this family responsibility to carry on the father's name demonstrated in a different way when we look at Chapter Four, discussing "Mahlah, Noah, Hoglah, Milcah, and Tirzah, Zelophehad's Daughters."

But the story of Lot's daughters uniting together to procreate with their father may have a different purpose, a literary one or even negative propaganda. For example, because the Moabites and Ammonites were too often fierce enemies with Israel over idols and property, some scholars such as Janice Nunnally-Cox, author of *Foremothers,* thinks that the telling of the incestuous circumstances of their birth was a way to demean these powerful opponents of Israel.

Finally, we do not know the details of these sisters' lives after their delivery of Moab and Ben-Ammi. It is likely that they remained close, because of the crisis they endured together and the demands of raising their sons without having husbands. These sisters certainly had survival spirits, willing to do whatever it took to keep the family going. These sisters may have enjoyed family life again, with their sons and daughters-in-law giving them grandchildren to surround them with affection and care for their needs in old age.

Lot's daughters present us with a challenge. We can see them as bad, because of their behavior with their father. Or we can see them as good, because of their obedience to God by not looking back at Sodom, staying with their father and caring for him through old age, and being in unity with one another by supporting one another. In addition, we have the option of seeing them as human—living their lives as best as they could. Even girls grow into women and learn from their life experiences.

Each of us are on our own life journey, making decisions which others will find fault with or even condemn us for making. But we have a free will to do what we believe is best at the time. We may not want to emulate every behavior of every woman we know or hear about—in or out of scripture. However, there is always something to learn from every experience and every person's life. The unity of Lot's daughters, regardless of how they used it, is one good behavior we can seek to acquire with one another.

Women more then men report that they need to feel really connected to those who are significant in their lives. Feeling really connected is feeling the Virtue of unity. It is gratifying for any individual to feel unity in some way with another human being. Sisterhood is one rewarding version of unity which crosses the lines of biology and legality. We can all learn to move closer to one another in a real unity of spirit and purpose by looking in the scriptures and around us every day for models of sisterhood and brotherhood. David and Jonathan shared the unity of brotherhood with one another. Ruth and Noami shared the unity of sisterhood with one another. With God's help, we can find and share with one another the unity of our sisterhood and brotherhood.

Lot's Daughters
Genesis 19:1-38

These two sisters lived with their mother and father, in Sodom. The night before they were forced to flee for their lives, their father, Lot, offered the virgin sisters to a crowd of men who were eager to rape the two visiting angels Lot had invited home for the night. The crowd refused the girls and were struck blind, leaving Lot's household alone. The angels sent Lot to warn the girls' fiancées to escape Sodom, but they thought he was joking. The next morning the angels took the family out of the city, warning them not to pause even for a brief look back or they would also be consumed. Their mother did and was! The sisters went with their father to Zoar and then he moved them to a cave in the hills. When their father was old, they made him drunk and each conceived his child.

Focus Virtue: Unity

*How very good and pleasant it is
when kindred live together in unity!*

Psalm 133:1

The unity of these sisters is clearly demonstrated by their ability to work together for their survival and perpetuation of the family. Women without a man were women who would perish. Like Lot's daughters, when we join forces with another person to focus on a goal, whether for survival or for success, we, too can accomplish what we set out to do. When we join together to accomplish something good, our good unites us with one another and at least lives on in us.

*I will let unity with others be guided by the
good we can accomplish together.*

Virtues Reflection: Lot's Daughters

When we look at Lot's daughters we are reminded that the sisters in the Bible are included in the scriptures for a variety of reasons—from which we can learn. When we look seriously at these sisters we can see Virtues to be admired and emulated, such as awareness, courageousness, and purposefulness. We can also see that these sisters displayed the need to exercise some of their Virtues and further develop other Virtues they had.

As you read, reflect, and discuss the stories of these sisters, Lot's daughters, what are the Virtues you identify in each of them? *(You may want to review the Focus Virtues list in Chapter One.)* Take a few moments to identify developed Virtues of each sister. Then complete the following exercise with them in mind.

Which one of the developed Virtues of the older sister do you most appreciate, today?

Which one of the developed Virtues of the younger sister do you most appreciate, today?

How have these Virtues been part of your life in the past or in the present?

How do you see these Virtues or the need for them in your life, now?

What can you do to further develop these Virtues in your life?

What have you found most interesting about this study?

Action Scripture

Luke 6:36-38 *Be merciful, just as your Father is merciful. Do not judge, and you will not be judged; do not condemn, and you will not be condemned. Forgive, and you will be forgiven; give, and it will be given to you. A good measure, pressed down, shaken together, running over, will be put into your lap; for the measure you give will be the measure you get back.*

Grateful Prayer

Mighty God, You are more powerful than anyone, than cities, than nature. But You are more than fair, You are merciful. We thank You for Your mercy which warns us of danger and tries to take us out of harms way. Now we ask that You grant us understanding of what may be harmful to us and grant us strength to turn and run from the danger, without looking back. Help us to be merciful to one another, to comfort one another, and to love one another—just as You have been merciful, have comforted, and have loved us. And bring us into unity with one another and with You. AMEN

Chapter Three

Leah & Rachel

Never mistake a kinship for a relationship.
Christine M. Carpenter

Leah & Rachel

> **Gen. 29:4-11** Jacob said to them, "My brothers, where do you come from?" They said, "We are from Haran." He said to them, "Do you know Laban son of Nahor?" They said, "We do." He said to them, "Is it well with him?" "Yes," they replied, "and here is his daughter Rachel, coming with the sheep." He said, "Look, it is still broad daylight; it is not time for the animals to be gathered together. Water the sheep, and go, pasture them." But they said, "We cannot until all the flocks are gathered together, and the stone is rolled from the mouth of the well; then we water the sheep." While he was still speaking with them, Rachel came with her father's sheep; for she kept them. Now when Jacob saw Rachel, the daughter of his mother's brother Laban, and the sheep of his mother's brother Laban, Jacob went up and rolled the stone from the well's mouth, and watered the flock of his mother's brother Laban. Then Jacob kissed Rachel, and wept aloud.

Why do you think Rachel was bringing the sheep to water that particular day?

a. The shepherd who watered the sheep was sick that day and she was just filling in for him.

b. She was trying to learn how to be a shepherdess and was making a short trip with her father's herd.

c. Her older sister did the domestic work and Rachel did the shepherding.

d. Other?

What do you think Rachel thought or felt when Jacob kissed her and wept aloud?

a. She was afraid of him, a stranger.

b. She wanted to know who he was and take him home with her to meet her family.

c. He made her heart sing.

d. Other?

> **Gen. 29:12-20** And Jacob told Rachel that he was her father's kinsman, and that he was Rebekah's son; and she ran and told her father. When Laban heard the news about his sister's son Jacob, he ran to meet him; he embraced him and kissed him, and brought him to his house. Jacob told Laban all these things, and Laban said to him, "Surely you are my bone and my flesh!" And he stayed with him a month. Then Laban said to Jacob, "Because you are my kinsman, should you therefore serve me for nothing? Tell me, what shall your wages be?" Now Laban had two daughters; the name of the elder was Leah, and the name of the younger was Rachel. Leah's eyes were lovely, and Rachel was graceful and beautiful. Jacob loved Rachel; so he said, "I will serve you seven years for your younger daughter Rachel." Laban said, "It is better that I give her to you than that I should give her to any other man; stay with me." So Jacob served seven years for Rachel, and they seemed to him but a few days because of the love he had for her.

How old do you think Rachel and Jacob were when they first met?

a. Both were teenagers.

b. Both were in their twenties.

c. Rachel was in her twenties and Jacob in his thirties.

d. Rachel was a young girl and Jacob was at least forty years old because his twin brother Esau had married at forty, already.

e. Other?

List the things you think Rachel and Leah shared with each other initially about their feelings and attractions for their cousin Jacob?

When a man demonstrated his love for you or his interest in you, how sensitive were you, with regard for the feelings of single women?

Leah & Rachel

> **Excerpts from Gen. 29:20-30** So Jacob served seven years for Rachel, and they seemed to him but a few days because of the love he had for her. Then Jacob said to Laban, "Give me my wife that I may go in to her, for my time is completed." So Laban gathered together all the people of the place, and made a feast. But in the evening he took his daughter Leah and brought her to Jacob; and he went in to her....When morning came, it was Leah! And Jacob said to Laban, "What is this you have done to me? Did I not serve with you for Rachel? Why then have you deceived me?" Laban said, "This is not done in our country—giving the younger before the firstborn. Complete the week of this one, and we will give you the other also in return for serving me another seven years." Jacob did so, and completed her week; then Laban gave him his daughter Rachel as a wife.... So Jacob went in to Rachel also, and he loved Rachel more than Leah.

Why did Leah agree to take the place of Rachel?

a. She loved Jacob from the first time she saw him.
b. She wanted to get married to anyone.
c. She was just obeying her father.
d. She wanted to spite and hurt her sister.
e. Other?

Why did Rachel let Jacob go in to Leah on their wedding night?

a. Her father had threatened to harm her if she told about the switch.
b. She thought Jacob would immediately discover the switch and send for her, instead.
c. She was taught to obey her father's wishes.
d. She was happy to share Jacob with her beloved sister.
e. Other?

All the Women in the Bible: Sisters & Sisterhood

> **Gen. 29:31-35** When the LORD saw that Leah was unloved, he opened her womb; but Rachel was barren. Leah conceived and bore a son, and she named him Reuben; for she said, "Because the LORD has looked on my affliction; surely now my husband will love me." She conceived again and bore a son, and said, "Because the LORD has heard that I am hated, he has given me this son also"; and she named him Simeon. Again she conceived and bore a son, and said, "Now this time my husband will be joined to me, because I have borne him three sons"; therefore he was named Levi. She conceived again and bore a son, and said, "This time I will praise the LORD"; therefore she named him Judah; then she ceased bearing.

What kind of sisters do you think Leah and Rachel were to one another *before* their marriages to Jacob?

a. Friends?   b. Competitors?

c. Helpers?   d. Conspirators?

e. Enemies?   f. Other?

What kind of sisters do you think Leah and Rachel were to one another *after* their marriages to Jacob?

a. Friends?   b. Competitors?

c. Helpers?   d. Conspirators?

e. Enemies?   f. Other?

How would you have felt toward your sister if you were Leah? Why?

How would you have felt toward your sister if you were Rachel? Why?

Leah & Rachel

> **Excerpts form Gen. 30:1-8** When Rachel saw that she bore Jacob no children, she envied her sister; and she said to Jacob, "Give me children, or I shall die!" Jacob became very angry with Rachel and said, "Am I in the place of God, who has withheld from you the fruit of the womb?". . . So she gave him her maid Bilhah as a wife; and Jacob went in to her. And Bilhah conceived and bore Jacob a son. Then Rachel said, "God has judged me, and has also heard my voice and given me a son"; therefore she named him Dan. Rachel's maid Bilhah conceived again and bore Jacob a second son. Then Rachel said, "With mighty wrestlings I have wrestled with my sister, and have prevailed"; so she named him Naphtali.

Why was it important to Rachel to bear children for her husband?

a. She saw herself only as a worthy human being according to how many sons she could produce.
b. Her status in the family was based upon her production of sons.
c. It was her duty to provide male heirs for her husband, and she understood her responsibility and wanted to fulfill it.
d. Other?

What was the nature of the sisterhood which existed between Rachel and her maid, Bilhah?

a. They were close friends and playmates from childhood.
b. They were like sisters and shared everything they had with one another.
c. They helped each other do everything.
d. They worked as a team in the home.
e. None, because slaves were tools to be used.
f. Other?

All the Women in the Bible: Sisters & Sisterhood

> **Excerpts from Gen. 30:14-24** In the days of wheat harvest Reuben went and found mandrakes in the field, and brought them to his mother Leah. Then Rachel said to Leah, "Please give me some of your son's mandrakes." But she said to her, "Is it a small matter that you have taken away my husband? Would you take away my son's mandrakes also?" Rachel said, "Then he may lie with you tonight for your son's mandrakes." When Jacob came from the field in the evening, Leah went out to meet him, and said, "You must come in to me; for I have hired you with my son's mandrakes." So he lay with her that night. And...she conceived and bore Jacob a fifth son. . . and she bore Jacob a sixth son...Afterwards she bore a daughter...Then God remembered Rachel, and ...opened her womb. She conceived and bore a son, and said, "God has taken away my reproach"; and she named him Joseph, saying, "May the LORD add to me another son!"

Why did Leah give her maid Zilpah to Jacob (Gen. 30:9-13) even after Leah had the most children?

a. Zilpah wanted to sleep with Jacob, too.

b. Jacob hinted that Rachel gave her maid to him, and so should Leah.

c. Leah did not want any doubt as to which wife supplied the most sons.

d. Rachel dared her to.

e. Other?

In the conversation about the mandrakes, what were the sisters really negotiating for and why?

a. Their husband, because they both wanted his love.

b. The mandrake root, because each wanted to use it to become fertile and have sons for Jacob.

c. Power, because each wanted to control her sister.

d. Other?

Leah & Rachel

Leah & Rachel's

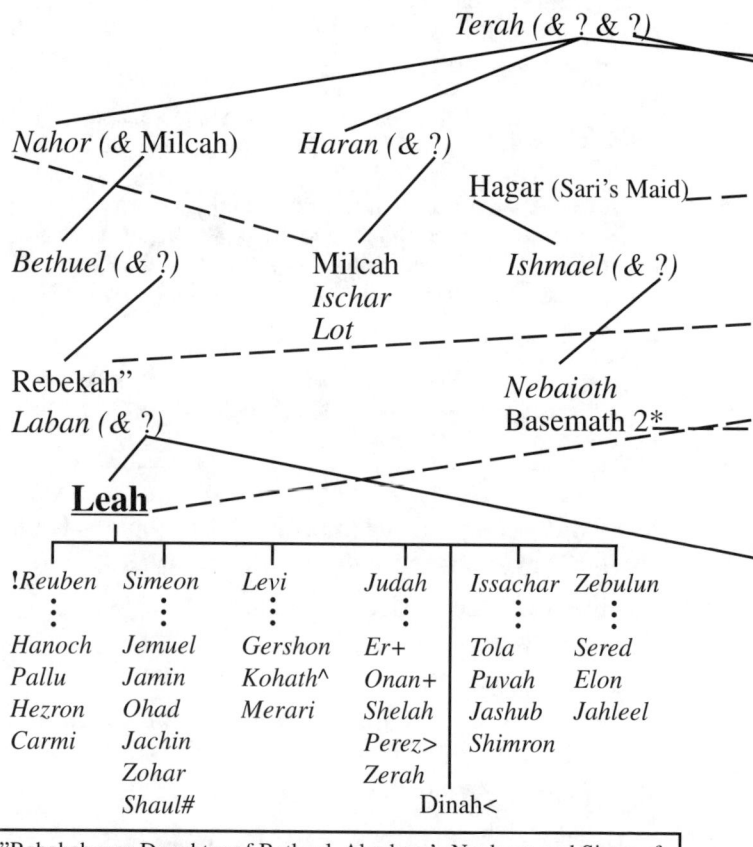

Terah (& ? & ?)

Nahor (& Milcah)   Haran (& ?)

Hagar (Sari's Maid)

Bethuel (& ?)   Milcah
                Ischar
                Lot

Ishmael (& ?)

Rebekah"   Nebaioth
Laban (& ?)   Basemath 2*

Leah

!Reuben	Simeon	Levi	Judah	Issachar	Zebulun
Hanoch	Jemuel	Gershon	Er+	Tola	Sered
Pallu	Jamin	Kohath^	Onan+	Puvah	Elon
Hezron	Ohad	Merari	Shelah	Jashub	Jahleel
Carmi	Jachin		Perez>	Shimron	
	Zohar		Zerah		
	Shaul#		Dinah<		

"Rebekah was Daughter of Bethuel, Abraham's Nephew; and Sister of Laban, Jacob's Uncle & Father-in-law
*Basemath 2 is also called Mahalath (Gen. 36:3; 28:9)
! Reuben laid with Bilhah, his father's concubine (Gen. 35:22)
#Shaul was the son of a Canaanite woman
^Kohath and his descendants continued the line of Priests of Israel
+Er and Onan died in the land of Canaan
>The children of Perez were Hezron and Hamul; In the linage of Jesus
<Dinah was dishonored by Shechem (see Gen. 34:1- 35:5)
=The children of Beriah were Heber and Malchiel
**Joseph's wife was Asenath, daughter of Potiphera, priest of On

All the Women in the Bible: Sisters & Sisterhood

Family Tree

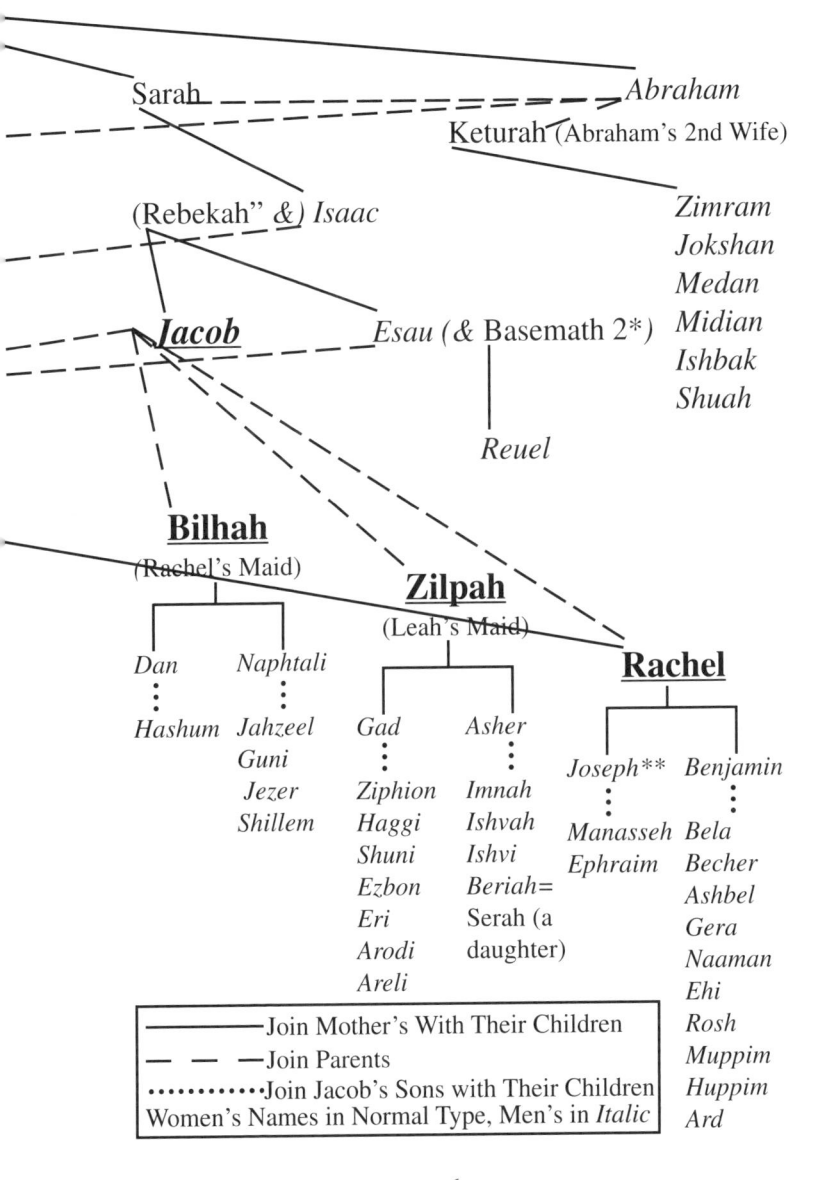

Sarah ———— Abraham
Keturah (Abraham's 2nd Wife)

(Rebekah" &) Isaac

Zimram
Jokshan
Medan
Midian
Ishbak
Shuah

Jacob — Esau (& Basemath 2*)

Reuel

Bilhah
(Rachel's Maid)

Zilpah
(Leah's Maid)

Rachel

Dan	Naphtali	Gad	Asher	Joseph**	Benjamin
Hashum	Jahzeel	Ziphion	Imnah	Manasseh	Bela
	Guni	Haggi	Ishvah	Ephraim	Becher
	Jezer	Shuni	Ishvi		Ashbel
	Shillem	Ezbon	Beriah=		Gera
		Eri	Serah (a		Naaman
		Arodi	daughter)		Ehi
		Areli			Rosh
					Muppim
					Huppim
					Ard

———— Join Mother's With Their Children
— — — Join Parents
·········· Join Jacob's Sons with Their Children
Women's Names in Normal Type, Men's in *Italic*

65

Wedding Traditions of the Times

During the time Leah and Rachel lived, traditions were usually meticulously followed. One tradition said that fathers had absolute control over their families and could sell any of their children into slavery if they were not obedient. In addition, fathers always arranged their daughters' marriages. Betrothal of marriage partners, even before birth, was made to benefit the families, often by acquisition of property, status, or a form of peace treaty. In most cases the daughter was not consulted about her father's choice of her husband. Some marriages were arranged the day the children were born. Often the wedding feast was the setting for the first meeting of the bride and groom. It was the custom of some tribes to marry their daughters off in succession, beginning with the eldest.

On their wedding day, brides stayed in seclusion and were heavily veiled from head to foot so that they would not be seen by their bridegroom until after their marriage. The bride's dress was made of pure white embroidery, glittering with all her family jewels and special gifts from her bridegroom. Her hair was perfumed and worn down over her shoulders. On her head was a wreath woven as a crown from myrtle. Her forehead shimmered with silver ornaments. Myrrh, aloes, and cassia fragrances emanated from her wedding garments. The "attrie" was a peculiar girdle always worn by the bride.

Over all her wedding garments she wore a heavily embroidered veil of betrothal that covered her so completely that she could not be seen through its embroidery. The veil of betrothal could not be lifted by her husband until after she had entered into his house or tent as his wife. The veil was symbolic of her subjection to her husband. (The custom was strict seclusion of a wife. A husband could divorce his wife if she went out on the street without being veiled.)

Oddly enough, the bride, being so wrapped in garments as to imitate a shroud, her orthodox wedding gift for her bridegroom was actually a shroud. He was required to wear it twice each year, first for New Year's day and then on the Day of Atonement. According to custom, widows were married on Fridays, virgins on Wednesdays. A favorite time to marry was March, being springtime, with flowers abounding and perfuming the air while birds sang.

The wedding feast lasted seven days. Only work that was absolutely necessary was done during the festivities. All preparations were to be done prior to the wedding feast. The entire community was invited and everyone dressed in their wedding garments. For one week everyone would celebrate the marriage by singing, dancing, socializing, eating, and drinking.

As was the custom, the marriage feast began with a heavily adorned bride waiting for her bridegroom to come and get her as she sat with her wedding party in the house of her father. At a time no one knew beforehand, the adorned, anointed bridegroom processed with his wedding party in loud gaiety from his house to her's. It could be getting dark and their torches would light the path as onlookers shouted their encouragement. The bride's attending maidens carried lighted lamps to meet the bridegroom's wedding party, joining in the singing and dancing greetings to the bride.

However, the bride never took part in the first day of the marriage feast. Instead, the bride stayed in a separate room, attended by her maidens. The bride remained shrouded by her betrothal veil and was not brought out until it was time for her to be taken to the bridegroom's tent.

There was no religious ceremony. What made it a legal marriage was "tenting the bride." Her father led her to the bridegroom's tent, with her maidens following in dance and song. The father placed his daughter's hand in the hand of the bridegroom. When the bridegroom accepted the bride and they entered the door of the tent together their marriage began. Only after they had closed the door of the tent could the husband remove his wife's veil, and symbolically throw it over his shoulder to demonstrate that her life would be upon his shoulders from now on. This was the marriage bond.

The bride and groom, now wife and husband, remained in seclusion together for the remaining week while the wedding guests "partied". It was the bridegroom who laid in store their supplies of food and drink for the wedding week. At the end of the wedding week the couple appeared for a final banquet with their guests.

Sisters Name Their Children

Genesis 29:32 **Leah** *conceived and bore a son, and she named him Reuben; for she said, "Because the LORD has looked on my affliction; surely now my husband will love me."*

Genesis 29:33 *She [**Leah**] conceived again and bore a son, and said, "Because the LORD has heard that I am hated, he has given me this son also"; and she named him Simeon.*

Genesis 29:34 *Again she [**Leah**] conceived and bore a son, and said, "Now this time my husband will be joined to me, because I have borne him three sons"; therefore he was named Levi.*

Genesis 29:35 *She [**Leah**] conceived again and bore a son, and said, "This time I will praise the LORD"; therefore she named him Judah; then she ceased bearing.*

Genesis 30:4-6 *So she [**Rachel**] gave him her maid Bilhah as a wife; and Jacob went in to her. And Bilhah conceived and bore Jacob a son. Then Rachel said, "God has judged me, and has also heard my voice and given me a son"; therefore she named him Dan.*

Genesis 30:7-8 **Rachel**'s *maid Bilhah conceived again and bore Jacob a second son. Then Rachel said, "With mighty wrestlings I have wrestled with my sister, and have prevailed"; so she named him Naphtali.*

Genesis 30:10-11 *Then **Leah**'s maid Zilpah bore Jacob a son. And Leah said, "Good fortune!" so she named him Gad.*

Genesis 30:12-13 **Leah**'s *maid Zilpah bore Jacob a second son. And Leah said, "Happy am I! For the women will call me happy"; so she named him Asher.*

Genesis 30:17-18 *And God heeded Leah, and she [Leah] conceived and bore Jacob a fifth son. Leah said, "God has given me my hire because I gave my maid to my husband"; so she named him Issachar.*

Genesis 30:19-20 *And* **Leah** *conceived again, and she bore Jacob a sixth son. Then Leah said, "God has endowed me with a good dowry; now my husband will honor me, because I have borne him six sons"; so she named him Zebulun.*

Genesis 30:21 *Afterwards she [Leah] bore a daughter, and named her Dinah.*

Genesis 30:22-24 *Then God remembered Rachel, and God heeded her and opened her womb. She [Rachel] conceived and bore a son, and said, "God has taken away my reproach"; and she named him Joseph, saying, "May the LORD add to me another son!"*

Genesis 35:16-18 *Then they journeyed from Bethel; and when they were still some distance from Ephrath,* **Rachel** *was in childbirth, and she had hard labor. When she was in her hard labor, the midwife said to her, "Do not be afraid; for now you will have another son." As her soul was departing (for she died), she named him Ben-oni; but his father called him Benjamin.*

Why Argue Over Mandrakes?

Mandrakes are mentioned in only two places in the Bible:

Genesis 30:14-16 *In the days of wheat harvest Reuben went and found mandrakes in the field, and brought them to his mother Leah. Then Rachel said to Leah, "Please give me some of your son's mandrakes." But she said to her, "Is it a small matter that you have taken away my husband? Would you take away my son's mandrakes also?" Rachel said, "Then he may lie with you tonight for your son's mandrakes." When Jacob came from the field in the evening, Leah went out to meet him, and said, "You must come in to me; for I have hired you with my son's mandrakes." So he lay with her that night.*

Song of Solomon 7:13 *The mandrakes give forth fragrance, and over our doors are all choice fruits, new as well as old, which I have laid up for you, O my beloved.*

Sources vary in their description of mandrakes. One source says that mandrakes are narcotic plants. Another identifies mandrakes as a plant that is sometimes called May apple. Still more specific is David Mace, author of *Hebrew Marriage,* saying that:

> From the most ancient time, aphrodisiac virtues have been ascribed to the mandrake,

which was therefore supposed to cure barrenness, and it is now known that the root, when eaten, would have the effect of relaxing the womb.

An additional source identifies mandrake as a plant with dark green leaves and small, yellow, sweet fruit that was often used medicinally. One final description of mandrake says that it is a poisonous plant of the nightshade family, found in Mediterranean regions. Further, its purple or white flowers top a short stem which sends down a forked thick root. Because its root resembled a human shape, it was thought to have magical powers and was also used for its narcotic and emetic results.

It appears that Rachel took seriously her wifely duty to produce sons for her husband Jacob. It was not enough that he had sons with her sister, Leah. Rachel's self worth required her to give Jacob sons from her. To fulfill her drive for acceptance as a fruitful wife, Rachel first went to her husband and begged him, *"Give me children, or I shall die"* (Genesis 30:1)! Jacob's response is revealing, about the attitudes of the times regarding unsuccessful baby producers. Genesis 30:2 says that *"Jacob became very angry with Rachel and said, 'Am I in the place of God, who has withheld from you the fruit of the womb?'"*

Immediately, seeking to give Jacob sons from her, Rachel did the only thing she knew to do. Following the example of Jacob's grandmother Sari/Sarah, who was Rachel's great-aunt, two generations before her.

> *"Then she [Rachel] said, 'Here is my maid Bilhah; go in to her, that she may bear upon my knees and that I too may have children*

through her. So she gave him her maid Bilhah as a wife; and Jacob went in to her. And Bilhah conceived and bore Jacob a son. Then Rachel said, "God has judged me, and has also heard my voice and given me a son"; therefore she named him Dan. Rachel's maid Bilhah conceived again and bore Jacob a second son. Then Rachel said, "With mighty wrestlings I have wrestled with my sister, and have prevailed"; so she named him Naphtali.

Genesis 30:3-8

It is important to remember that the custom of the day held women in esteem not according to their skills or beauty as much as it did according to their production of sons. Perhaps the same is true today. Sons meant a great deal to husbands. Sons inherited the family's material worth and carried on the family name. Sons were expected to keep alive the family traditions and also honor their fathers who came before them.

Women who could not bear sons for their husbands were often considered cursed or punished by God. Even centuries later, history records many a Queen banished or even beheaded for her inability to produce male progeny. Interestingly enough, it was not until after Rachel bargained the mandrakes away from her sister Leah that Rachel actually conceived and gave birth to Joseph, her firstborn.

Jacob's Past Affected Everyone's Future

Isaac, the son of Abraham and Sarah, was forty years old when he married his first cousin once removed, Rebekah, daughter of Bethuel the Aramean of Paddan-aram. Rebekah was the sister of Laban the Aramean, who would later become Jacob's father-in-law. Rebekah had been barren, but her husband, Isaac, prayed that she would conceive. According to biblical record, her pregnancy was not a pleasant one, and as a result, the LORD responded to her maternity inquiry by saying that: "Two nations are in your womb, and two peoples born of you shall be divided; the one shall be stronger than the other, the elder shall serve the younger" (Genesis 25:23). When the twins were born, the first came out "red, all his body like a hairy mantle." They named him Esau. Jacob came out gripping Esau's heel. Esau was a skillful hunter and a man of the field, therefore, because Isaac was fond of game he loved his firstborn son, Esau. On the other hand, Jacob was a quiet man, living in tents near his mother, therefore Rebekah loved Jacob.

Once, when Jacob was cooking a stew, Esau came in from the field, saying, "Let me eat some of that red stuff, for I am famished!"

Jacob bargained, "First sell me your birthright."

Esau reasoned, "I am about to die; of what use is a birthright to me?"

Jacob said, "Swear to me first." So he swore to him, and sold his birthright to Jacob and he gave Esau bread and lentil stew.

When Esau was forty years old, he married Judith and Basemath, daughters of Hittites. They made life bitter for Isaac and Rebekah. Later Esau married again, taking a wife from his father's people. Her name was

Basemath, also. But this second Basemath was the daughter of Ishmael, son of Hagar and Abraham.

When Isaac was old and felt death near, he called his elder son Esau and told him to go out to the field, and hunt game for Isaac to eat, so that Isaac could bless Esau before Isaac died. Rebekah heard the plan and told Jacob to bring two choice kids from the flock, and she would prepare them as savory food for his father, so that Isaac would bless Jacob, instead, before Isaac died. Jacob did as his mother said and she put the skins of the kids on his hands and on the smooth part of his neck and Jacob impersonated his brother Esau. Isaac could not see well enough to tell the difference between his two sons, so Isaac was tricked into giving the blessing to Jacob instead of Esau his firstborn son.

Afterward, when Rebekah heard Esau plotting to kill Jacob because Esau lost his birthright, she persuaded Isaac to bless Jacob and send him away to safety to Paddan-aram, to Laban son of Bethuel the Aramean, her brother who was Jacob's uncle. There Jacob met and fell in love with Rachel, but was tricked by Laban into marrying her elder sister, Leah, also. While he worked for Laban among his flocks, Jacob fathered children by both wives, Leah and Rachel, and their two maid servants, Bilhah and Zillpah. After approximately twenty years, Jacob was ready to return home and called his wives to discuss it.

Jacob told them that their father had cheated him and changed his wages ten times. It was the LORD who was telling Jacob to leave this land at once and return to the land of his birth. Rachel and Leah concurred with Jacob and said they were ready to leave their father's house because he was treating them like foreigners—their father had sold them (to Jacob) and was using up the money given for them. They wanted their share of their father's money for themselves and for their children. Therefore Leah and Rachel agreed to do whatever the LORD said to Jacob.

While Laban was out sheering the sheep, Jacob took his children and wives on camels, all the property that he had gained, all the livestock in his possession that he had acquired in Paddan-aram, and set out to go to his father Isaac in the land of Canaan.

Without Jacob knowing it, Rachel stole her father's household gods, idols which were believed to bring good fortune, such as fertility. On the third day after the band had departed, Laban was told that Jacob had fled with his family and goods. Laban pursued Jacob, catching him seven days later, in the hills of Gilead.

But before Laban could overtake Jacob, God told Laban, "Take heed that you say not a word to Jacob, either good or bad." So when Laban overtook Jacob he asked him why he had secretly fled? Then he asked Jacob why he stole the household gods? Jacob told Laban that he was afraid of him, but that he had not stolen the gods. When Laban searched for the idols he did not find them because Rachel had put them in the camel's saddle, and sat on them—claiming she could not get up because it was her womanly time of the month. Laban and Jacob parted in peace, but Jacob's peace was short lived.

As the band approached Canaan, Jacob sent word to Esau, the brother Jacob had cheated out of his birthright, saying, *"Your servant Jacob, 'I have lived with Laban as an alien, and stayed until now; and I have oxen, donkeys, flocks, male and female slaves; and I have sent to tell my lord, in order that I may find favor in your sight"* (Genesis 32:4-5).

Soon the messengers reported that Esau was coming with four hundred men to meet Jacob. Putting his wives maids and their children at the front, Jacob arranged his family in marching order. Leah and her children were next, and Rachel and Joseph were last.

Jacob was afraid and sent a present to his brother Esau: two hundred female goats and twenty male goats, two hundred ewes and twenty rams, thirty milch camels and their colts, forty cows and ten bulls, twenty female donkeys and ten male donkeys. Jacob went before his family and bowed himself to Esau and appeased him with humble words and many gifts. Esau refused Jacob's peace offerings but accepted his brother home in peace. However, Jacob insisted that Esau take the gifts and Esau reluctantly complied with Jacob's wishes. The crisis passed and Jacob journeyed on with his family, to a place apart from where his brother was living.

If there had been any doubt before, each family member now knew the worth Jacob put on him or her. By his arrangement of marching order, with the maids and their children in front, then Leah and her children, and finally, Rachel and Joseph, all knew their place in Jacob's heart.

Throughout his life Jacob flaunted his favoritism for Rachel and her children. It is no wonder that as Joseph grew up without his mother, but a doting father, Joseph was hated by his older brothers who had shielded Joseph from potential danger and death the day they marched to meet Esau. Joseph was the inheritor of his father's good intentions toward him, but also the inheritor of the seeds of jealousy and hatred that Jacob help plant in his own sons toward their brother Joseph. Later, Jacob's sons conspire against Joseph and sell him into a life of difficulty in Egypt.

Final Resting Places

Genesis 35 records that after appeasing Esau, the family journeyed to Bethel where the LORD appeared to Jacob, changing his name to Israel. As the group moved on from Bethel, still some distance from Ephrath, Rachel was in childbirth, having hard labor. As she was dying, her midwife told Rachel that she was having a son. Rachel named him Ben-oni, which means "son of my sorrow." But his father, Jacob, called him Benjamin, which means the "son of the right hand"—the right hand being the position of greatest honor. Rachel died, and was buried on the way to Ephrath (Bethlehem). Jacob set up a pillar at her grave, which is said to be there to this day.

Genesis 49 tells us that Jacob buried Leah in the family plot—in the cave in the field of Ephron the Hittite, in the cave in the field at Machpelah, near Mamre, in the land of Canaan, in the field that Abraham bought from Ephron the Hittite as a burial site. It also records that the Cave of Machpelah near Hebron in Canaan was where Abraham and his wife Sarah were buried, as well as where Isaac and his wife Rebekah were buried. Jacob would join Leah there later, as his final resting place. Norah Lofts, author of *Women in the Old Testament,* writes:

> ...the story ends with a curious twist....Was it a sense of family, of tribal tradition that made him choose to lie there, rather than at Bethlehem with the woman whom he had loved? Or was Leah's right as the first wife thus asserted and Rachel acknowledged to be a thing apart, a romantic, unprofitable

diversion from the tribal path?...was there, in the dust, a stirring, a sense of final triumph? Once, long ago Leah had bargained for one night of love; now the last, the longest night of all, was hers.

Genesis 49 also recounts Jacob's burial instructions to his sons. Joseph had his father embalmed by the physicians. The process took forty days, and the Egyptians wept for Jacob seventy days. When they were done weeping Joseph asked Pharaoh to help him take his father's body back to the resting place of Jacob's choice—in the land of Canaan. Pharaoh granted Joseph's request and also sent all the servants of Pharaoh, the elders of his household, and all the elders of the land of Egypt, as well as all the household of Joseph, his brothers, his father's household, chariots and charioteers—a very great company. They left their children, their flocks, and their herds in the land of Goshen. When they arrived at the burial site, the time of mourning for Jacob was seven days with very great and sorrowful lamentation. When the burial and mourning were completed, all the participants returned to Egypt.

According to Dr. William H. Shea, an inscription has been found in Egypt which appears to be an eyewitness account of the procession taking Jacob's body back to the Cave of Machpelah near Hebron in Canaan. Shea believes the time to be during the reign of Sesostris III. The records of that time tell of participation in a campaign into Canaan, with many camels and Egyptians in caravan. Because Egypt had no known enemies or battles in Canaan during this time, Shea believes the campaign referred to is the expedition sent to bury Jacob.

Reflection

Women in competition with one another for the same man is a popular theme in literature, theater, television, and movies. Sisters in competition with one another for the same man is an even more intriguing theme. But when the gals are not competing on paper, stage, over the airwaves, or on the big screen, then it can be really damaging to both the participants and the observers. In the case of Leah and Rachel, we see them competing quite intently.

Leah was competing for the love and admiration of her husband, Jacob. Her need to feel love from her husband was reflected in the naming of her firstborn son, Reuben. *"Leah conceived and bore a son, and she named him Reuben; for she said, 'Because the LORD has looked on my affliction; surely now my husband will love me'"* (Genesis 29:32). As the scriptures record, Leah did not find the love she needed from Jacob. *"She [Leah] conceived again and bore a son, and said, 'Because the LORD has heard that I am hated, he has given me this son also'; and she named him Simeon"* (Genesis 29:33). It would be too late for Leah, but some time later, the Apostle Paul would give clear instructions to husbands to love their wives—perhaps for reasons similar to this.

Even in the face of adversity and all that must have gone with feeling unloved and even hated, Leah did not give up trying to win her husband's love. She still sought to be really connected to him and *"Again she [Leah] conceived and bore a son, and said, 'Now this time my husband will be joined to me, because I have borne him three sons'; therefore he was named Levi"* (Genesis 29:34).

After the fourth son was born, however, Leah was

waning in determination and she stopped bearing children. It is possible that she stopped sharing her bed with Jacob. Or, perhaps Rachel monopolized all of Jacob's baby-making time.

With four sons to Leah's credit, eventually, Rachel gave her maid to Jacob to get children for her to give to Jacob. Rachel's maid, Bilhah, bore two sons from her unions with Jacob and they were accounted as Rachel's children. With Rachel getting help to build her family of sons for Jacob, Leah became inspired once again to become involved in the baby boy race as she saw her record of four sons in jeopardy of being lost to Rachel's team. Therefore, Leah gave Jacob her maid, Zilpah, who bore two more sons to Leah's credit.

However, Leah did not let Jacob stay out of her bed forever. In fact, with some mandrakes Reuben had brought to his mother, Leah bought Jacob's bedroom services from Rachel. As a result Leah was back in the child bearing business with a fifth son of her flesh, and then a sixth (Genesis 30:19-20):

> *"And Leah conceived again, and she bore Jacob a sixth son. Then Leah said, 'God has endowed me with a good dowry; now my husband will honor me, because I have borne him six sons'; so she named him Zebulun."*

Even though Leah physically bore six sons from her own body, plus two from her maid, did Leah ever get the affection she so desperately wanted from Jacob? It appears that even though Leah had many sons she must not have received the kind of love she wanted, because the scriptures say that she still wanted her husband's love. Contrariwise, Rachel had the love of her husband but still wanted many sons. Although she had two sons for Jacob, through her maid, Rachel continued to crave the bearing of sons for Jacob through her own body. In the end, her desire to be accepted for her production of male progeny cost Rachel her life in bearing her second child, Benjamin.

When we look at the story of these sisters, we are not just looking back in time at Leah and Rachel in their struggle over Jacob and his pleasure, approval, and love. We are also looking into today and the way women compete for men: to make them happy, to have them appreciate us, and to really feel loved by them. It is interesting to note that Jacob in this story and perhaps men today are not hurt in the same way that women are by the competition for love and approval by the object of their affections—and some say that men may even enjoy it when women compete for their affections! However, we must ask ourselves: What does competition between sisters cost women, their children, their men, and other sisters? What price are we willing to pay, or make others pay, so that we may win the competition of daily life: the positive self-esteem race, the power/control/leadership race, the best of the baby race, and the desirable sexual partner race?

What could our relationships be like if instead of competing for ego, position, possession, and affection, we competed to love one another in spirit and in truth? Loving and being loved are vital expressions of our humanity and our spirituality. When we love in spirit and in truth we are truly human and truly spiritual. It is our nature, the nature created in the image and likeness of God, to love. We may not be able to get all the loving we want but we can give all the love we want to the women in our lives, too!

Leah

Genesis 29:16, 23-25, 30-32; 30:9, 11, 13-14, 16-20; 31:4, 14; 33:1-:2, 7; 34:1; 35:23; 46:15-18; 49:31; Ruth 4:11

Leah's father agreed to let Jacob marry Leah's younger sister, Rachel, but instead brought a heavily veiled Leah to Jacob's tent. The next morning Jacob discovered the trick but was coerced into keeping Leah and adding Rachel as a second wife. Jacob did not love Leah as he loved Rachel, and Leah knew it. In spite of Jacob's favoritism, Leah was a willing wife and bore Jacob six sons, plus two more from her maid, Zilpah. Leah was a faithful, eager, supportive wife always longing for her husband's love.

Focus Virtue: Honor

Let love be genuine; hate what is evil, hold fast to what is good; love one another with mutual affection; outdo one another in showing honor.

Romans 12:9-10

Leah said she felt hated, but she still did what was right and kept her marriage agreement. Even though her husband did not give her the love she wanted, she continued to be his wife and eagerly bore his children. She held her place in the family, with dignity and honor, regardless of what others did or said. We also live with honor, if we live with respect for what we have agreed to, and fulfill what is right. If we are unashamed of being a good example of what is just in whatever circumstances we find ourselves, we will be honoring ourselves, others, and God.

I will respect myself and others by honoring my word and being a good example of integrity.

Rachel

Genesis 29:6, 9-12, 29:16-18, 20, 25, 28-31;
30:1- 2, 6, 8, 14-15, 22, 25; 31:4, 14, 19, 32, 34;
33:1, 7; 35:16, 19, 24; 46:19, 22, 25; 48:7;
Ruth 4:11; Jeremiah 31:15; Matthew 2:18

Rachel was loved by Jacob, her husband, but she could not conceive. In an effort to give her husband children from her, she gave her maid to Jacob, and Bilhah bore two sons. However, Rachel was not satisfied with the surrogate births from her maid, so she continued to try to conceive a child of her own to present to Jacob. One time she bartered with her sister for Mandrakes in order to conceive—and she did. Rachel died in childbirth delivering her second son.

Focus Virtue: Determination

But if someone stands firm in his[her] resolve, being under no necessity but having his[her] own desire under control, and has determined in his[her] own mind to . . . [s]he will do well.

1Corinthians 7:37

Rachel had set a goal for herself. She believed that it was important for her to have children and was determined to give her husband sons from her, even if it meant getting a surrogate mother to help. Rachel asked for help from her husband, her sister, and her maid. She kept going even when the going got tough and tougher. When we use our willpower to focus our energy on a task until it is completed, no matter how difficult or how long it takes, our determination can make even the impossible happen for us and others.

I will use purposeful determination to focus my energy on my goals until they are achieved.

Virtues Reflection: Leah & Rachel

Leah and Rachel are reminders that the sisters in the Bible are included in the scriptures for a variety of reasons—but all worth understanding. These biblical sisters demonstrate Virtues to be admired and emulated by us, such as obedience, responsibility, and willingness. They also show the need to exercise their Virtues more consistently and further develop some of their Virtues.

While you read, reflect, and discuss the stories of these sisters, Leah and Rachel, think about which Virtues you identify in each of them. *(You may want to review the Focus Virtues list in Chapter One.)* Spend a few minutes to identify and focus on the developed Virtues of Leah and the developed Virtues of Rachel. Then complete the following exercise with Leah and Rachel in mind.

Which one of the developed Virtues of Leah do you most appreciate, today?

Which one of the developed Virtues of Rachel do you most appreciate, today?

How have these Virtues been part of your life in the past or in the present?

How do you see these Virtues or the need for them in your life, now?

What can you do to further develop these Virtues in your life?

What has helped you most about this Bible sister story, their Focus Virtues or this reflection?

Action Scripture

1John 4:20-21 *Those who say, "I love God," and hate their brothers or sisters, are liars; for those who do not love a brother or sister whom they have seen, cannot love God whom they have not seen. The commandment we have from him is this: those who love God must love their brothers and sisters also.*

Grateful Prayer

Loving Spirit, be with us now as we pause to sense Your presence and let You hold us in Your arms of love. Caress us with Your gentleness that we may be gentle with others. Breathe on us Your breath of life that we may be sources of life to others. Whisper to us words of encouragement that we may be encouragers of others. Guide us into all truth that we may lead others to You and Your truth, in love. Show us how to honor one another and give us the determination to do what You show us. AMEN

Chapter Four

Mahlah, Noah, Hoglah, Milcah, & Tirzah (Zelophehad's Daughters)

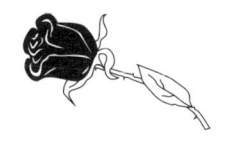

Sisterhood evokes geometric courage.
Christine M. Carpenter

Mahlah, Noah, Hoglah, Milcah, & Tirzah

> **Num. 26:33-34** Now Zelophehad son of Hepher had no sons, but daughters: and the names of the daughters of Zelophehad were Mahlah, Noah, Hoglah, Milcah, and Tirzah. These are the clans of Manasseh; the number of those enrolled was fifty-two thousand seven hundred.
>
> **Excerpts from Num. 27:1-4** Then the daughters of Zelophehad came forward. . . They stood before Moses, Eleazar the priest, the leaders, and all the congregation, at the entrance of the tent of meeting, and they said, "Our father died in the wilderness; he was not among the company of those who gathered themselves together against the LORD in the company of Korah, but died for his own sin; and he had no sons. Why should the name of our father be taken away from his clan because he had no son? Give to us a possession among our father's brothers."

Why were Zelophehad's daughters the first women we hear about who spoke up for their inheritance?

a. No one thought of it before!
b. The others who spoke up before were ignored and gave up.
c. These sisters knew who to go to at the right time.
d. These five beautiful sisters got attention wherever and whenever they appeared together.
e. Others were heard before, but no one recorded their requests because they did not get anything and nothing changed.
f. Other?

What do you think the sisters did to prepare themselves for their presentation before Moses, Eleazar the priest, the leaders, and all the congregation?

If you were one of Zelophehad's daughters, what would you have done to prepare yourself and your sisters for presenting your case before Moses?

> **Num. 27:5-11** Moses brought their case before the LORD. And the LORD spoke to Moses, saying: The daughters of Zelophehad are right in what they are saying; you shall indeed let them possess an inheritance among their father's brothers and pass the inheritance of their father on to them. You shall also say to the Israelites, "If a man dies, and has no son, then you shall pass his inheritance on to his daughter. If he has no daughter, then you shall give his inheritance to his brothers. If he has no brothers, then you shall give his inheritance to his father's brothers. And if his father has no brothers, then you shall give his inheritance to the nearest kinsman of his clan, and he shall possess it. It shall be for the Israelites a statute and ordinance, as the LORD commanded Moses."

After hearing their case, why did Moses take the matter of Zelophehad's daughters' inheritance before the LORD?

a. He thought the LORD would confirm the current policy on property inheritance, which did not include daughters.
b. He brought every matter presented to him before the LORD.
c. He wanted the sisters to get a piece of the Promised Land.
d. He wanted to be fair to everyone and did not know what was the right thing to do for the sisters.
e. Other?

If the LORD knew that what the daughters of Zelophehad were requesting was right, then why did the LORD wait for the sisters to speak up and present their case to those in authority over them before righting the wrong that had prevailed for generations of fathers without sons?

Mahlah, Noah, Hoglah, Milcah, & Tirzah

> **Num. 36:1-3** The heads of the ancestral houses of the clans of the descendants of Gilead son of Machir son of Manasseh, of the Josephite clans, came forward and spoke in the presence of Moses and the leaders, the heads of the ancestral houses of the Israelites; they said, "The LORD commanded my lord to give the land for inheritance by lot to the Israelites; and my lord was commanded by the LORD to give the inheritance of our brother Zelophehad to his daughters. But if they are married into another Israelite tribe, then their inheritance will be taken from the inheritance of our ancestors and added to the inheritance of the tribe into which they marry; so it will be taken away from the allotted portion of our inheritance . .

Why did Moses let the heads of the ancestral houses of the clans bring additional requirements of inheritance for Zelophehad's daughters?

a. He did not know what they were going to say until it was too late.
b. He listened to what all the heads of the ancestral houses had to say.
c. He knew that additional requirements were needed.
d. He knew that the biological—genetic—divine mandate to financial generosity within families needed to be addressed more specifically.
e. Other?

What do you think about these additional conditions on the sisters' inheritance?

What would you have said to the leaders about the additional requirements they put on after the LORD had spoken?

> **Num. 36:5-9** Then Moses commanded the Israelites according to the word of the LORD, saying, "The descendants of the tribe of Joseph are right in what they are saying. This is what the LORD commands concerning the daughters of Zelophehad, 'Let them marry whom they think best; only it must be into a clan of their father's tribe that they are married, so that no inheritance of the Israelites shall be transferred from one tribe to another; for all Israelites shall retain the inheritance of their ancestral tribes. Every daughter who possesses an inheritance in any tribe of the Israelites shall marry one from the clan of her father's tribe, so that all Israelites may continue to possess their ancestral inheritance.

Why did the sisters keep silent about the additional restrictions on their inheritance?

a. They were happy to get inheritance rights of any kind, under any conditions.

b. They were afraid of the heads of the ancestral houses of the clans.

c. They wanted to marry among their own people anyway so to them it was not a restriction at all.

d. They wanted to confer before they spoke up again, but never did get a chance to talk about it together.

e. They were told it was the commandment from the LORD.

f. The sisters were not present when the leaders made their case before Moses and no one told them about it.

g. Other?

How far do you think the sisters would have gone to inherit a part of the Promised Land?

What have you conceded to receive your request?

Mahlah, Noah, Hoglah, Milcah, & Tirzah

> **Num. 36:10-13** The daughters of Zelophehad did as the LORD had commanded Moses. Mahlah, Tirzah, Hoglah, Milcah, and Noah, the daughters of Zelophehad, married sons of their father's brothers. They were married into the clans of the descendants of Manasseh son of Joseph, and their inheritance remained in the tribe of their father's clan. These are the commandments and the ordinances that the LORD commanded through Moses to the Israelites in the plains of Moab by the Jordan at Jericho.

Why did the sisters marry their cousins?

a. They wanted to keep the inheritance in their own family.
b. They wanted to appease their uncles who were upset about not getting their brother's inheritance.
c. Their cousins wooed them relentlessly, in order to get the sisters' inheritance added on to their own.
d. They wanted to stay as close together as possible, and marrying their cousins accomplished this.
e. It was the only way they could receive their inheritance.
f. Other?

How far are you willing to go to receive what you ask for?

At what point would you speak out against unreasonable or unjust requirements or restrictions attached to granting your request?

How far are you willing to go to speak up for justice, or against injustice, for either yourself or for your biological or spiritual sisters?

> **Excerpts from Josh. 17:2-6** And allotments were made to the rest of the tribe of Manasseh, by their families...these were the male descendants of Manasseh son of Joseph, by their families. Now Zelophehad son of Hepher son of Gilead son of Machir son of Manasseh had no sons, but only daughters.... They came before the priest Eleazar and Joshua son of Nun and the leaders, and said, "The LORD commanded Moses to give us an inheritance along with our male kin." So according to the commandment of the LORD he gave them an inheritance among the kinsmen of their father. Thus there fell to Manasseh ten portions, besides the land of Gilead and Bashan, which is on the other side of the Jordan, because the daughters of Manasseh received an inheritance along with his sons. The land of Gilead was allotted to the rest of the Manassites.

Why did the sisters have to ask again for their property?

a. It had been so long since the LORD had granted the sisters their inheritance that the people had really forgotten about it.

b. All the sisters had married men from their own clan so no one thought they really cared anymore about an inheritance in their father's name.

c. Their husbands made them ask again, since they were inheritors—insisting their wives get the property to add to the family plot.

d. The tribe did not want to institute the new law from the LORD, unless they absolutely had to.

e. No one wanted them to implement the new inheritance laws for fathers without sons.

f. Other?

Share about a time when you did speak up with or for yourself or for your biological or spiritual sisters.

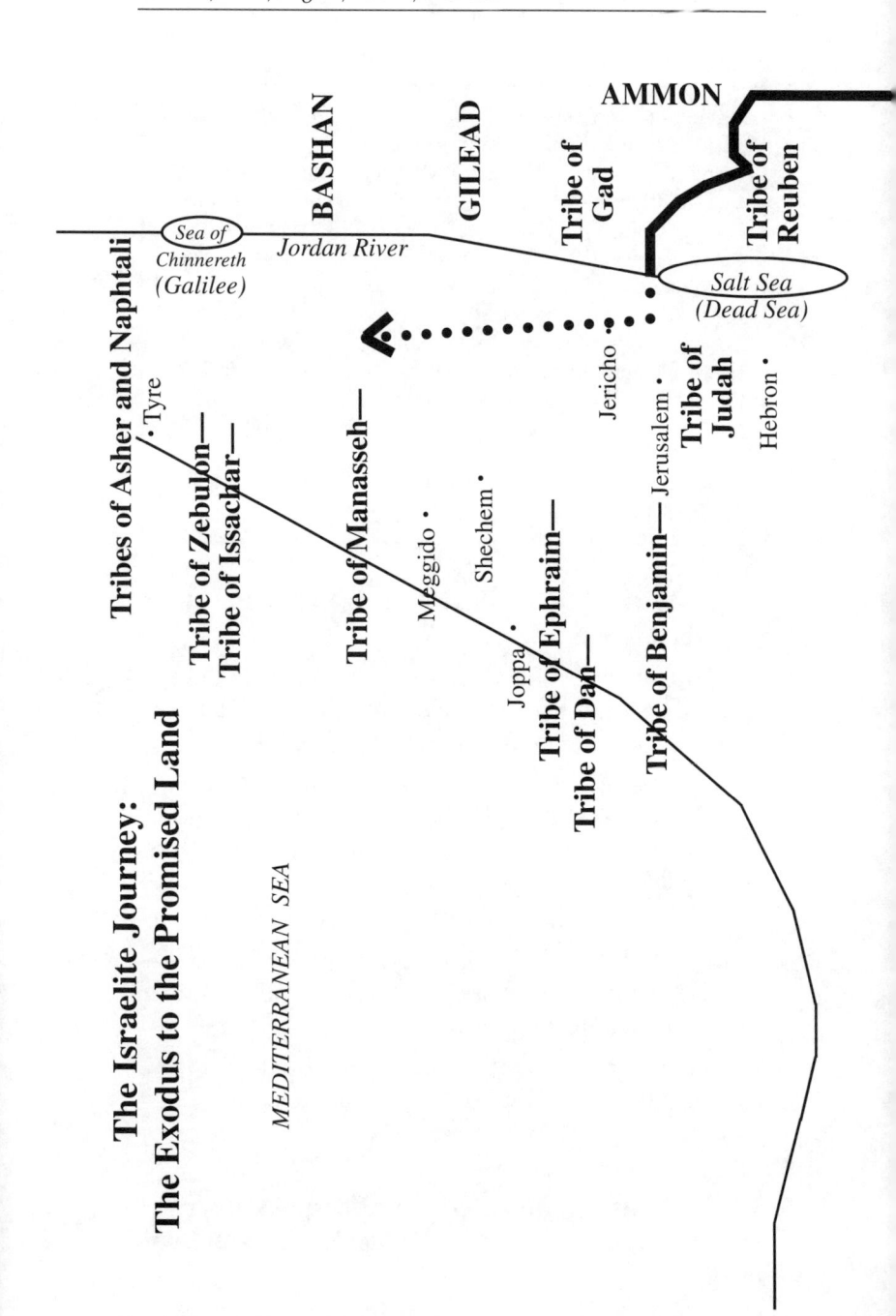

The Israelite Journey: The Exodus to the Promised Land

Map showing the tribes of Israel in the Promised Land:

- **AMMON**
- **BASHAN**
- **GILEAD**
- Tribe of Gad
- Tribe of Reuben
- Tribes of Asher and Naphtali
- Tribe of Zebulon
- Tribe of Issachar
- Tribe of Manasseh
- Tribe of Ephraim
- Tribe of Dan
- Tribe of Benjamin
- Tribe of Judah

Bodies of water and landmarks:
- Sea of Chinnereth (Galilee)
- Jordan River
- Salt Sea (Dead Sea)
- MEDITERRANEAN SEA
- Tyre
- Meggido
- Shechem
- Joppa
- Jericho
- Jerusalem
- Hebron

All the Women in the Bible: Sisters & Sisterhood

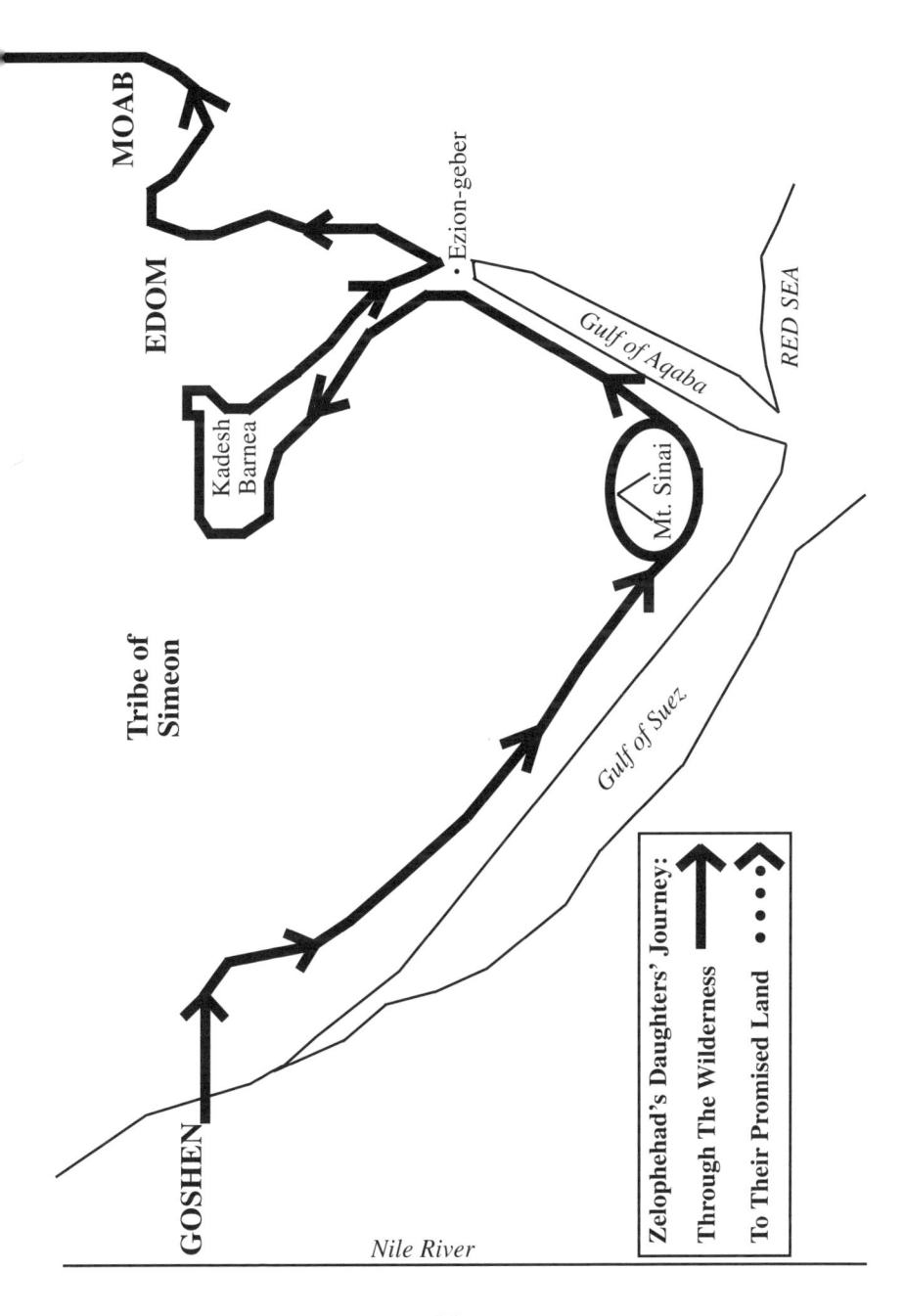

MOAB

EDOM

Ezion-geber

Gulf of Aqaba

RED SEA

Kadesh Barnea

Mt. Sinai

Tribe of Simeon

Gulf of Suez

Zelophehad's Journey:
Through The Wilderness ⬆
To Their Promised Land ⇧•••

GOSHEN

Nile River

Summary of the Wilderness Rebellions

After a successful exodus from Egypt and Pharaoh's tyranny, the Hebrew people grew weary from their wandering. When Moses sent spies to the land of Canaan, the spies returned with the report that the land "flows with milk and honey." However, that was the good news. The bad news was that the people in the land were as giants and the Hebrew people compared themselves to mere grasshoppers.

After weeping all night from fear, the people cried out to Moses and Aaron, saying, "Would that we had died in Egypt!" Joshua and Caleb were the only two spies who spoke positively about the land. But the congregation did not want to hear the favorable encouragement of Joshua and Caleb, therefore the people wanted to stone them in order to silence them.

However, the glory of the LORD appeared to all the people who saw the light of the Holy Presence. Being angry at their unbelief in God's ability to give them the land, the LORD wanted to disinherit Israel. But Moses begged for their forgiveness. Because of the words spoken by Moses, the LORD pardoned the people. As their punishment for unbelief, the LORD restricted their entrance into the Promised Land. Of those who were older than twenty years, only Joshua and Caleb were allowed to enter the new land. Therefore, the people were sentenced to wander in the wilderness for forty more years, until each who had rebelled in unbelief died.

Even though the people repented of their unbelief and rebellion, they continued to wander and fight among themselves. When three men, Korah, Dathan, and Abiram, rose up against Moses and Aaron, they were able to enlist hundreds of discontents to join them in their accusations towards their leaders. Again the LORD was ready to destroy all the congregation, but Moses begged for their lives, reminding the LORD that it was not like the LORD to kill the innocent along with the guilty. Then the LORD punished the rebels and all came to a bitter end. They lost their lives along with their wives, children, and possessions as the earth opened up and swallowed them all. In addition, fire came down and consumed 250 men offering the incense on behalf of the rebellious men and their cause.

The next day, the remaining congregation rose up against Moses and Aaron, and were stricken with a plague of death. But the plague was stopped when Aaron went to the middle of the congregation where the plague had begun, and offered incense, making atonement for the people. Fourteen thousand seven hundred people died from the plague, alone.

When the plague was stopped, the LORD instructed Moses to get a staff from each of the twelve leaders of their ancestral houses. Each man's name was written on his staff, and Aaron's name was put on the staff of Levi. Then all staffs were put in the tent of meeting before the covenant, where Moses met the LORD. It was decreed that the staff which sprouted would indicate who was the leader among the ancestral houses—ending all rebellion towards the leaders.

The next day, the staff of Aaron for the house of Levi had sprouted with buds, produced blossoms, and bore ripe almonds. Moses returned all staffs to their owners, showing Aaron's sprouted staff. Because of this, Aaron was declared undisputed leader. Then Aaron's staff was returned to the tent of meeting before the covenant, with the understanding that any further rebellion would result in the death of the instigators and the participants.

More Details About Some Rebellions

Excerpts from Num. 13:26-14:10a

And they came to Moses and Aaron and to all the congregation of the Israelites in the wilderness...and showed them the fruit of the land. And they told him, "...it flows with milk and honey, and this is its fruit. Yet the people who live in the land are strong, and the towns are fortified and very large..."But Caleb quieted the people before Moses, and said, "Let us go up at once and occupy it, for we are well able to overcome it." Then the men who had gone up with him said, "We are not able to go up against this people, for they are stronger than we....a land that devours its inhabitants; and all the people that we saw in it are of great size....and to ourselves we seemed like grasshoppers, and so we seemed to them." Then all the congregation raised a loud cry, and the people wept that night. And all the Israelites complained against Moses and Aaron; the whole congregation said to them, "Would that we had died in the land of Egypt! Or would that we had died in this wilderness! Why is the LORD bringing us into this land to fall by the sword? Our wives and our little ones will become booty; would it not be better for us to go back to Egypt?" So they said to one another, "Let us choose a captain, and go back to Egypt." Then Moses and Aaron fell on their faces before all the assembly of the congregation of the Israelites. And Joshua son of Nun and Caleb son of Jephunneh, who were among those who had spied out the land, tore their clothes and said to all the congregation of the Israelites, "The land...is an exceedingly good land. If the LORD is pleased with us, he will bring us into this land and give it to us...Only, do not rebel against the LORD; and do not fear the people of the land, for they are no more than bread for us; their protection is removed from them, and the LORD is with us; do not fear them." But the whole congregation threatened to stone them.

Ponder: How do you think this story affected the sisters' decision to approach Moses and Aaron?

Excerpts from Num. 14:10b-24
Then the glory of the LORD appeared at the tent of meeting to all the Israelites. And the LORD said to Moses, "How long will this people despise me? And how long will they refuse to believe in me, in spite of all the signs that I have done among them? I will strike them with pestilence and disinherit them, and I will make of you a nation greater and mightier than they." But Moses said to the LORD, "Then the Egyptians will hear of it...and they will tell the inhabitants of this land. They have heard that You, O LORD, are in the midst of this people; for You, O LORD, are seen face to face, and Your cloud stands over them and You go in front of them, in a pillar of cloud by day and in a pillar of fire by night. Now if You kill this people all at one time, then the nations who have heard about You will say, 'It is because the LORD was not able to bring this people into the land He swore to give them that He has slaughtered them in the wilderness.' And now, therefore, let the power of the LORD be great in the way that You promised when You spoke, saying, The LORD is slow to anger, and abounding in steadfast love, forgiving iniquity and transgression, but by no means clearing the guilty, visiting the iniquity of the parents upon the children to the third and the fourth generation.' Forgive the iniquity of this people according to the greatness of Your steadfast love... Then the LORD said, "I do forgive, just as you have asked; nevertheless... none of the people who have seen my glory and the signs that I did in Egypt and in the wilderness, and yet have tested me these ten times and have not obeyed my voice, shall see the land that I swore to give to their ancestors; none of those who despised me shall see it. But my servant Caleb, because he has a different spirit and has followed me wholeheartedly, I will bring into the land into which he went, and his descendants shall possess it.

Ponder: How did the preceding story of rebellion and forgiveness affect the sisters' concept of: Moses, Aaron, Joshua, Caleb, a just God?

Mahlah, Noah, Hoglah, Milcah, & Tirzah

Excerpts from Num. 16:1-35
Now Korah...along with Dathan and Abiram...and On...took two hundred fifty Israelite men, leaders of the congregation...and they confronted Moses. They assembled against Moses and against Aaron, and said to them, "You have gone too far! All the congregation are holy, everyone of them, and the LORD is among them. So why then do you exalt yourselves above the assembly of the LORD?" When Moses heard it, he fell on his face. Then he said to Korah and all his company, "In the morning the LORD will make known who is his, and who is holy, and who will be allowed to approach him.... Do this: take censers, Korah and all your company, and tomorrow put fire in them, and lay incense on them before the LORD; and the man whom the LORD chooses shall be the holy one. You Levites have gone too far!...Is it too little for you that the God of Israel has separated you from the congregation of Israel, to allow you to approach him in order to perform the duties of the LORD's tabernacle, and to stand before the congregation and serve them?...What is Aaron that you rail against him?"...Then Korah assembled the whole congregation against them at the entrance of the tent of meeting. And the glory of the LORD appeared to the whole congregation. Then the LORD spoke to Moses and to Aaron, saying: Separate yourselves from this congregation, so that I may consume them in a moment. They fell on their faces, and said, "O God, the God of the spirits of all flesh, shall one person sin and you become angry with the whole congregation?" And the LORD spoke to Moses, saying: Say to the congregation: Get away from the dwellings of Korah, Dathan, and Abiram....As soon as he finished speaking all these words, the ground under them [Korah, Dathan, and Abiram] was split apart. The earth opened its mouth and swallowed them up, along with their households —everyone who belonged to Korah and all their goods. And fire came out from the LORD and consumed the two hundred fifty men offering the incense.

Ponder: Knowing this story, why would the sisters take the chance of being thought of as rebelling?

Excerpts from Num. 16:41-17:10
On the next day, however, the whole congregation of the Israelites rebelled against Moses and against Aaron, saying, "You have killed the people of the LORD." And when the congregation had assembled against them, Moses and Aaron turned toward the tent of meeting; the cloud had covered it and the glory of the LORD appeared...and the LORD spoke to Moses, saying, "Get away from this congregation, so that I may consume them in a moment." And they fell on their faces. Moses said to Aaron, "Take your censer, put fire on it from the altar and lay incense on it, and carry it quickly to the congregation and make atonement for them. For wrath has gone out from the LORD; the plague has begun." So Aaron took it as Moses had ordered, and ran into the middle of the assembly, where the plague had already begun among the people. He put on the incense, and made atonement for the people. He stood between the dead and the living; and the plague was stopped. Those who died by the plague were fourteen thousand seven hundred, besides those who died in the affair of Korah. When the plague was stopped...The LORD spoke to Moses, saying: Speak to the Israelites, and get twelve staffs from them, one for each ancestral house, from all the leaders of their ancestral houses. Write each man's name on his staff, and write Aaron's name on the staff of Levi. For there shall be one staff for the head of each ancestral house. Place them in the tent of meeting before the covenant, where I meet with you. And the staff of the man whom I choose shall sprout; thus I will put a stop to the complaints of the Israelites that they continually make against you....When Moses went into the tent of the covenant on the next day, the staff of Aaron for the house of Levi had sprouted. It put forth buds, produced blossoms, and bore ripe almonds...and they looked, and each man took his staff. And the LORD said to Moses, "Put back the staff of Aaron before the covenant, to be kept as a warning to rebels, so that you may make an end of their complaints against me, or else they will die."

Ponder: Do you think that others thought the sisters were rebels against the law and tradition of Israel?

Selected Female Role Models of the Time

Puah & Shiphrah
Midwives who defied Pharaoh's orders and did not kill all male Hebrew babies at birth. (Exodus 1:15)

Jochebed
She defied Pharaoh's orders and kept her child, Moses, alive until he could be adopted by Pharaoh's daughter. (Exodus 6:20)

Miriam
As a child and adult she defied Pharaoh's orders and risked her life to protect and support her brother Moses. (Exodus 15:20)

Zipporah
Wife of Moses who became the circumcisor of their two sons, to fulfill the commandment of the LORD. (Exodus 2:21)

Elisheba
Wife and mother of the men who were the first Hebrew priests, their descendents continuing the priesthood. (Exodus 6:23)

Mahlah, Noah, Hoglah, Milcah, & Tirzah
(Numbers 26:33)

Rahab
A harlot who defied the King of Jericho and instead of turning over the Hebrew spies to the authorities, she hid them in her house. (Joshua 2:1)

Achsah
Daughter of Caleb given to her uncle as a military prize, asked her father for land and springs, and received both. (Joshua 15:16)

The Ark of the Covenant & God

Mahlah, Noah, Hoglah, Milcah, and Tirzah stood at the entrance to the tent of meeting. Why did they meet their leaders at that location to make their request? Was it because the sisters knew that the LORD was wherever the Ark of the Covenant was and that they had confidence that if the LORD heard their request, then they would have justice? What was this ark that became synonymous with God?

Exodus 25 tells us that the LORD instructed Moses to make an ark of acacia wood, two and a half cubits long, a cubit and a half wide, and a cubit and a half high. It was to have an overlay of pure gold, inside and out, as well as a molding of gold all around. There were to be four rings of gold put on its four feet, two rings on opposite sides. The poles to be put through the rings to carry the ark were to be of acacia wood, overlaid with gold, and never removed.

The LORD gave Bezalel and Oholiab (and others) special skill to make all He commanded Moses: the tent of meeting; the ark of the covenant; the mercy seat that is on it; all the furnishings of the tent; the table and its utensils; the pure lampstand with all its utensils; the altar of incense; the altar of burnt offering with all its utensils; the basin with its stand; the finely worked vestments; the holy vestments for the priest, Aaron, and the vestments of his sons, for their service as priests; the anointing oil and the fragrant incense for the holy place.

On the first day of the first month Moses was to set up the tabernacle of the tent of meeting: putting in it the ark of the covenant, screening the ark with the curtain; then came the table, its setting; the lampstand and lamps; the golden altar for incense before the ark of the covenant; the screen for the entrance of the tabernacle; the altar of burnt offering before the entrance of the tabernacle of the tent of meeting; the basin between the tent of meeting and the altar, with water in it; the court set up all around, and; the screen that would hang up as a gate of the court.

The LORD spoke to Moses from the entrance of the tent of meeting. Offerings to the LORD were brought to the entrance of the tent of meeting, where the congregation assembled. Roy Lee DeWitt, in *Teaching from the Tabernacle*, says that the ark was synonymous with God. For example, look at excerpts from 1Samuel 4:5-22:

> *When the ark of the covenant of the LORD came into the camp, all Israel gave a mighty shout, so that the earth resounded. When the Philistines...learned that the ark of the LORD had come to the camp, the Philistines were afraid; for they said, "Gods have come into the camp." They also said, "Woe to us! For nothing like this has happened before. Woe to us! Who can deliver us from the power of these mighty gods? These are the gods who struck the Egyptians with every sort of plague in the wilderness. Take courage, and be men, O Philistines, in order not to become slaves to the Hebrews as they have been to you; be men and fight." So the Philistines fought; Israel was defeated, and they fled, everyone to his home. There was a very great slaughter, for there fell of Israel thirty thousand foot soldiers. The ark of God was captured...A man of Benjamin ran from the battle line, and came to Shiloh the same day, with his*

clothes torn and with earth upon his head....Then the man came quickly and told Eli.... "Israel has fled before the Philistines, and there has also been a great slaughter among the troops; your two sons also, Hophni and Phinehas, are dead, and the ark of God has been captured." When he mentioned the ark of God, Eli fell over backward from his seat by the side of the gate; and his neck was broken and he died, for he was an old man, and heavy. He had judged Israel forty years. Now his daughter-in-law, the wife of Phinehas, was pregnant, about to give birth. When she heard the news that the ark of God was captured, and that her father-in-law and her husband were dead, she bowed and gave birth; for her labor pains overwhelmed her. As she was about to die...named the child Ichabod, meaning, "The glory has departed from Israel," because the ark of God had been captured and because of her father-in-law and her husband. She said, "The glory has departed from Israel, for the ark of God has been captured."

At the least the Ark of the Covenant was to contain the two tablets with the Ten Commandments, the budded rod of Aaron's, and the manna once used to feed the Israelites in the wilderness. Rabbi Chaim Richman, executive director of the Temple Institute in Jerusalem says that the ark symbolized the presence of God, the Shekinah glory. The authors of *Where Is the Lost Ark?*, Doug Wead, David Lewis, and Hal Donaldson, believe that the ark was also a symbol to the Israelites. The ark symbolized the pledge of the presence of God, through which God audibly spoke.

While the Ark of the Covenant is believed to be the most sacred object in Judaism, it has been likened to Egyptian and Babylonian religious arks. One proponent of this theory is Jordan Maxwell, coauthor of *The Book Your Church Doesn't Want You to Read.* Maxwell, a southern California mythology educator, asserts that:

> IS was the personification of Isis, the feminine wisdom. RA was for the Sun, and EL was for God. So they inculcated these religious movements and used the ark of the covenant for religious ceremony only in the story and only for morality.
> The story of the ark is a very ancient story in the Semitic world. It goes all the way back to the Babylonians, the Assyrians, the Persians, the Greeks, the Egyptians. All of those ancient Semitic cultures had a story of an ark of the covenant. The Egyptians had the most important ark, for that is where the Hebrew ark is borrowed from.

Refuting this type of criticism is Bible teacher, Don Steward, author of *In Search of the Lost Ark.* Steward acknowledges ancient analogies to the ark in model temples, tent-shrines, chariots for gods, squared thrones, and coffins for gods. However, he contends that other cultures only superficially resemble the Hebrew ark. In addition, he believes many of the similar arks came along after the Hebrew ark. Most important, the Hebrew ark, unlike the arks in other cultures, is associated with supernatural events and power.

Reflection

At first glance, it appears that the story of these assertive sisters who banded together, united to attain justice, is one of strength, hope, and success. However, that is just the surface reading of these scripture passages. Yes, in the end, even with the afterthought of marital limitations, these women still have acquired property through God-given inheritance rights. In addition, they have secured these rights for their daughters after them.

However, when we look more closely, we may see a picture that is not as fulfilling or encouraging as initially thought. For example, what reason was given by the sisters for their interest in inheriting property? The answer is clearly stated in their first request, before Moses, saying, *"...Why should the name of our father be taken away from his clan because he had no son?"* Whether the sisters used the idea that they wanted to perpetuate their father's name, or whether that was the only reason they wanted inheritance rights along with the males of the clan, they received the rights they requested. So why not be happy? Once again, when we look at this victory for these women in this perspective, it is diluted by the perpetuation of male rights, not rights for females. How so?

As was the custom of the day in Hebrew patriarchal society, men were the only legal inheritors of property, real and personal. For example, a son inherited his father's land, flocks, and concubines. In addition, a brother even inherited his sister-in-law if she had not yet produced an heir for her deceased husband—which the surviving brother would provide!

When a man was unfortunate enough to not produce any male progeny to inherit his property, it was thought that his name died when he did. Even today, some folks link male heirs with the continuation of their name. Perhaps that is why it is more difficult for some than for others to accept the recent trend in blended names—when husband and wife hyphenate both last names to form one new name to bestow upon their children. However, this story may be seen as hopeful for any father who does not have a son. His daughters are legally, under this provision, his inheritors, responsible for perpetuating his name.

When the sisters in this story married sons of their father's brothers, their cousins, they were eligible for their inheritance. Although, not automatically, because the sisters had to ask Joshua for their inheritance a second time, when the Promised Land was being divided among the twelve tribes. In addition, the question arises, as to whether the daughter's inheritance was then seen as her husband's land, or even seized by her husband—thus forfeiting any continuance of her father's name, as was the stated purpose of the inheritance.

In any case, when it was time for the next step in inheritance, did the sons or daughters of Zelophehad's daughters inherit their grandfather's land? The truth is, it appears that the daughter was only a temporary stopgap in the inheritance chain for male property rights. In fact, inheritance is so rare among women of Bible times that when it occurs special mention is made of it. For example, in Judges 1:12-15, Caleb gives his daughter, Achsah, property and water, the springs of Upper Gulloth and Lower Gulloth, when she asks him—assertively—for them as a present upon her marriage to her uncle who won her as a military prize.

Women have a history of having to ask for what

they want, even when it is legally or morally theirs and possibly is long overdue. In addition, when the rightful requests of women are granted, too often women are so grateful that they fail to recognize that something is usually taken away at the same time. In some cases women forfeit their freedom of choice, because restrictions or limitations are placed upon them that are not placed upon the men who have the same right(s). At other times, women have had to accept their new found right(s) along with the blatant attacks on their femininity, intelligence, or self-respect.

Unfortunately, women in the time of Exodus were not given the same rights and respect equal to men. How regretful for any one at any time to have to settle for being viewed as less than any one else—in rights and respect. Elizabeth Cady Stanton, author of *The Woman's Bible,* commented, regarding the heads of the ancestral clans, saying that:

> They seemed to consider these noble women destitute of the Virtue of patriotism, of family pride, of all the tender sentiments of friendship, kindred and home, and so with their usual masculine arrogance they passed laws to compel the daughters of Zelophehad to do what they probably would have done had there been no law to that effect.

As we reflect on the assertive actions of these sisters we can see that we have positive role models to emulate. Just as with them, the LORD will also be there for us when we are assertive to right a wrong—for ourselves or for others! God's power is within us and will confirm our right to step forward in confidence and speak our requests to our leaders.

Mahlah
Numbers 26:33; 27:1; 36:11; Joshua 17:3

Mahlah was the sister of Noah, Hoglah, Milcah, and Tirzah, the five daughters of Zelophehad. Their father had no sons, so his daughters went to Moses, in the presence of the priest and leaders, to ask for their father's portion of the Promised Land to be given to them in his name. The LORD told Moses that the sisters were right in what they were asking and for the first time women were given the legal right of inheritance. Later they had to speak up again to remind Aaron of their inheritance rights, and received them.

Focus Virtue: Assertiveness

So they remained for a long time, speaking boldly for the Lord, who testified to the word of his grace by granting signs and wonders to be done through them.

Acts 14:3

In their assertiveness Mahlah and her sisters spoke boldly for what they believed was right. As a result, they received what they asked for and helped women in the same situation have the same rights from that time forward. When we speak boldly for what is right we are speaking on behalf of the LORD to state the case to right a wrong affecting ourselves and others. Just as these sisters received what was right from the LORD, even though it had never been done before, God's grace can change our world for the better when we assertively ask for what is right, even though it has never been done before.

With God's help and my boldness, I will be assertive when I am aware of a wrong that needs to be made right.

Virtues Reflection: Mahlah, Noah, Hoglah, Milcah, & Tirzah (Zelophehad's Daughters)

Again, we are reminded that the sisters in the Bible are able to teach us a variety of things. These sisters, Zelophehad's daughters, teach us about Virtues that are to be admired and emulated, such as confidence, hopefulness, and unity. They also teach us about our need to exercise our Virtues, assertively. In addition, these sisters demonstrate that the need for further development of our Virtues is important because what we do or do not do affects our sisters.

Today, when you read about, think on, and discuss the stories of these sisters, Mahlah, Noah, Hoglah, Milcah, and Tirzah (Zelophehad's daughters), identify the developed Virtues you see in them. *(You may want to review the Focus Virtues list in Chapter One.)* Then take a few moments to complete the following exercise with them in mind.

Which one of the developed Virtues of Mahlah, Noah, Hoglah, Milcah, and Tirzah do you most appreciate, today?

How has this Virtue been part of your life in the past or in the present?

How do you see this Virtue or the need for it in your life, now?

What can you do to further develop this Virtue in your life?

What has been the most valuable part of this study?

Action Scripture

Matthew 25:34-40 *Then the king will say to those at his right hand, 'Come, you that are blessed by my Father, inherit the kingdom prepared for you from the foundation of the world; for I was hungry and you gave me food, I was thirsty and you gave me something to drink, I was a stranger and you welcomed me, I was naked and you gave me clothing, I was sick and you took care of me, I was in prison and you visited me.' Then the righteous will answer him, 'Lord, when was it that we saw you hungry and gave you food, or thirsty and gave you something to drink? And when was it that we saw you a stranger and welcomed you, or naked and gave you clothing? And when was it that we saw you sick or in prison and visited you?' And the king will answer them, 'Truly I tell you, just as you did it to one of the least of these who are members of my family, you did it to me.'*

Grateful Prayer

Mighty God, You are a powerful God. We thank You for righting wrongs for Your people. We ask for understanding of what needs to be changed in our lives, and the courage to be assertive and step forward and ask for it. May those we ask, seek and find Your wisdom as they render Your word to us. Grant us grace to receive Your wisdom and guidance for whatever changes are ahead of us. AMEN

Chapter Five

Martha & Mary

*Sisters are under no obligation
to give us what we expect.*
Christine M. Carpenter

Martha & Mary

> **Luke 10:38-42** Now as they went on their way, he entered a certain village, where a woman named Martha welcomed him into her home. She had a sister named Mary, who sat at the Lord's feet and listened to what he was saying. But Martha was distracted by her many tasks; so she came to him and asked, "Lord, do you not care that my sister has left me to do all the work by myself? Tell her then to help me." But the Lord answered her, "Martha, Martha, you are worried and distracted by many things; there is need of only one thing. Mary has chosen the better part, which will not be taken away from her."

How did Martha get her home?

a. She inherited it from her deceased husband who had no heirs.
b. It was not really her home, but just where she lived with her brother and sister.
c. She bought it with money she earned serving as a domestic worker for others.
d. Other?

Why did Martha invite Jesus into her home?

a. She believed in the Hebrew tradition and instruction to entertain strangers—all strangers.
b. She was a prominent woman in Bethany and wanted to lend her endorsement to Jesus and his ministry.
c. Her home was always open to the Jews and it was customary for her to welcome spiritual teachers.
d. She was curious about the new religious teaching she heard from Jesus and wanted to learn more.
e. Other?

Why did Jesus defend Mary in the Luke 10 passage?

> **Excerpts from John 11:1-6** Now a certain man was ill, Lazarus of Bethany, the village of Mary and her sister Martha. Mary was the one who anointed the Lord with perfume and wiped his feet with her hair; her brother Lazarus was ill. So the sisters sent a message to Jesus, "Lord, he whom you love is ill." But when Jesus heard it, he said, "This illness does not lead to death; rather it is for God's glory, so that the Son of God may be glorified through it." Accordingly, though Jesus loved Martha and her sister and Lazarus, after having heard that Lazarus was ill, he stayed two days longer in the place where he was.
> **John 11:17-20** When Jesus arrived, he found that Lazarus had already been in the tomb four days. Now Bethany was near Jerusalem, some two miles away, and many of the Jews had come to Martha and Mary to console them about their brother. When Martha heard that Jesus was coming, she went and met him, while Mary stayed at home.

Why did Mary stay at home (John 11:20)?

Why did Martha get up and go to meet Jesus?

a. Martha was the older sister and responsible for speaking for her siblings.
b. Martha was too eager to talk with Jesus to sit and wait for him to come to her.
c. Meeting him was showing her respect for Jesus.
d. Other?

Why did the Jerusalem Jews come two miles to Bethany to console Martha and Mary?

a. Martha was a leader in her community.
b. Lazarus was a well respected man in Israel.
c. Mary was taking the loss very hard.
d. They heard that Jesus had been called and wanted to see him.
e. Other?

Martha & Mary

> **John 11:21-27** Martha said to Jesus, "Lord, if you had been here, my brother would not have died. But even now I know that God will give you whatever you ask of him." Jesus said to her, "Your brother will rise again." Martha said to him, "I know that he will rise again in the resurrection on the last day." Jesus said to her, "I am the resurrection and the life. Those who believe in me, even though they die, will live, and everyone who lives and believes in me will never die. Do you believe this?" She said to him, "Yes, Lord, I believe that you are the Messiah, the Son of God, the one coming into the world."

How did Martha talk to Jesus in John 11:21-27?

•Posture: •Tone:

•Volume: •Facial Expression:

•Words: •Other:

Why did Martha talk to Jesus the way she did in John 11:21-27?

a. Martha was angry at Jesus and this was her way of showing it.
b. Martha was following the customary bantering used in similar situations.
c. Martha had real questions she needed answered, so she spoke honestly from her heart.
d. Martha liked to talk out her feelings and Jesus had always been willing to be a good sounding-board for her.
e. Other?

How had Martha come to know and believe that Jesus was the Messiah, the Son of God, the one coming into the world?

> **John 11:28-33** When she had said this, she went back and called her sister Mary, and told her privately, "The Teacher is here and is calling for you." And when she heard it, she got up quickly and went to him. Now Jesus had not yet come to the village, but was still at the place where Martha had met him. The Jews who were with her in the house, consoling her, saw Mary get up quickly and go out. They followed her because they thought that she was going to the tomb to weep there. When Mary came where Jesus was and saw him, she knelt at his feet and said to him, "Lord, if you had been here, my brother would not have died." When Jesus saw her weeping, and the Jews who came with her also weeping, he was greatly disturbed in spirit and deeply moved.

Why did Martha go and get Mary and tell her that, "The Teacher is here and is calling for you," when the scriptures do not say Jesus was calling for Mary?

Why were the Jews sticking close to Mary and not following after Martha?

How were Mary's and Martha's encounters with Jesus different?

- Physical stance:
- Opening statement:

- Attitude:
- Response of Jesus:

- Sister's reaction:
- Jesus' reaction:

- Result
- Other:

How would you have handled the situation if you were Martha? If you were Mary? If you were Jesus?

Martha & Mary

> **John 11:34-45** He said, "Where have you laid him?" They said to him, "Lord, come and see." Jesus began to weep. So the Jews said, "See how he loved him!" But some of them said, "Could not he who opened the eyes of the blind man have kept this man from dying?" Then Jesus, again greatly disturbed, came to the tomb. It was a cave, and a stone was lying against it. Jesus said, "Take away the stone." Martha, the sister of the dead man, said to him, "Lord, already there is a stench because he has been dead four days." Jesus said to her, "Did I not tell you that if you believed, you would see the glory of God?" So they took away the stone. And Jesus looked upward and said, "Father, I thank You for having heard me. I knew that You always hear me, but I have said this for the sake of the crowd standing here, so that they may believe that You sent me." When he had said this, he cried with a loud voice, "Lazarus, come out!" The dead man came out, his hands and feet bound with strips of cloth, and his face wrapped in a cloth. Jesus said to them, "Unbind him, and let him go." Many of the Jews therefore, who had come with Mary and had seen what Jesus did, believed in him.

Why did Martha tell Jesus that there was a stench from the tomb?

a. She wanted him to be prepared for the odor.
b. She was still stuck in the physical reality of the situation and had not moved into the spiritual reality of the resurrection of her brother.
c. She wanted to rub it in that Jesus took too long, causing them to grieve four days without him.
d. It was her way of saying that it would be harder to bring Lazarus back to life than if he had just died.
e. Other?

What do you think of the reaction of Jesus to Martha's warning?

> **John 12:1-8** Six days before the Passover Jesus came to Bethany, the home of Lazarus, whom he had raised from the dead. There they gave a dinner for him. Martha served, and Lazarus was one of those at the table with him. Mary took a pound of costly perfume made of pure nard, anointed Jesus' feet, and wiped them with her hair. The house was filled with the fragrance of the perfume. But Judas Iscariot, one of his disciples (the one who was about to betray him), said, "Why was this perfume not sold for three hundred denarii and the money given to the poor?" (He said this not because he cared about the poor, but because he was a thief; he kept the common purse and used to steal what was put into it.) Jesus said, "Leave her alone. She bought it so that she might keep it for the day of my burial. You always have the poor with you, but you do not always have me."

What was Martha doing while Mary anointed Jesus?

Why did Jesus defend Mary in the John 12 passage?

a. He wanted to teach the disciples to honor him, even if it cost them dearly.
b. He knew how important it was to Mary for him to receive her gift.
c. He knew that this was a symbolic act of Mary's, accepting him as her Divine Bridegroom by anointing him with the ointment customarily used by the bride on her wedding night.
d. He knew that Judas was jealous of Mary's attention to him.
e. Other?

How were Martha and Mary good sisters to one another?

How could you be good to a sister, this week?

Martha & Mary

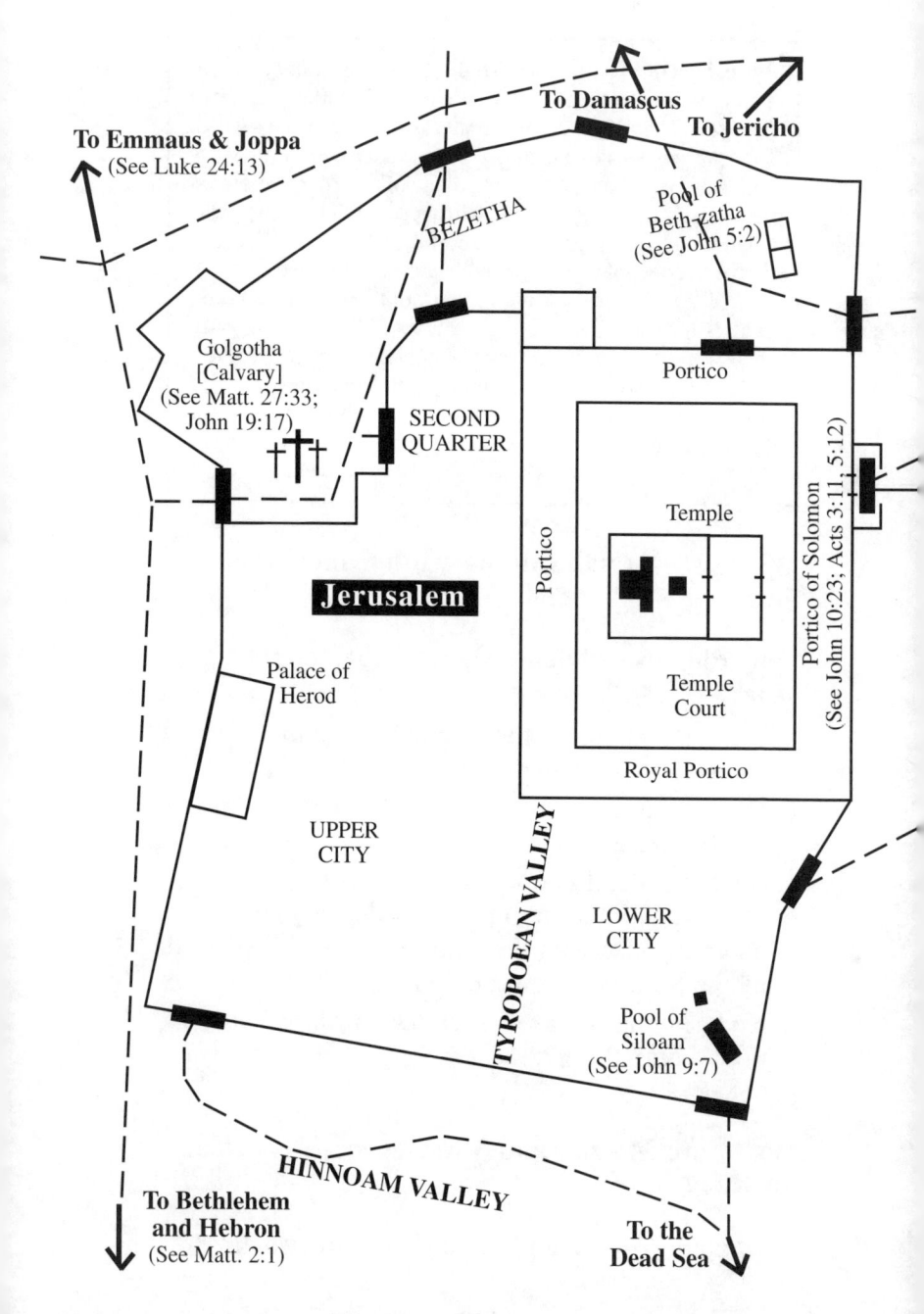

To Emmaus & Joppa
(See Luke 24:13)

To Damascus

To Jericho

BEZETHA

Pool of Beth-zatha
(See John 5:2)

Golgotha [Calvary]
(See Matt. 27:33; John 19:17)

SECOND QUARTER

Portico

Portico

Temple

Portico of Solomon
(See John 10:23; Acts 3:11, 5:12)

Jerusalem

Palace of Herod

Temple Court

Royal Portico

UPPER CITY

TYROPOEAN VALLEY

LOWER CITY

Pool of Siloam
(See John 9:7)

HINNOAM VALLEY

To Bethlehem and Hebron
(See Matt. 2:1)

To the Dead Sea

All the Women in the Bible: Sisters & Sisterhood

Map of Jerusalem and Vicinity
20 B.C. - 70 A.D.

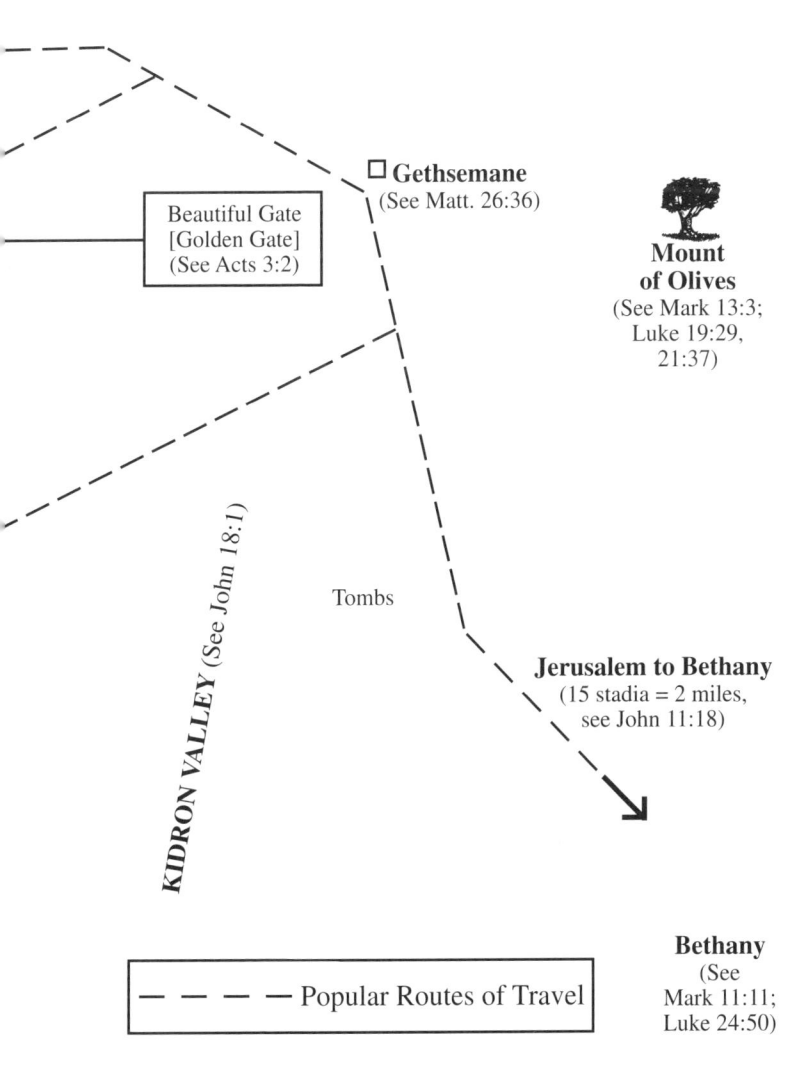

☐ **Gethsemane**
(See Matt. 26:36)

Mount of Olives
(See Mark 13:3; Luke 19:29, 21:37)

Beautiful Gate [Golden Gate]
(See Acts 3:2)

KIDRON VALLEY (See John 18:1)

Tombs

Jerusalem to Bethany
(15 stadia = 2 miles, see John 11:18)

– – – – Popular Routes of Travel

Bethany
(See Mark 11:11; Luke 24:50)

The Times & Traditions

The Jewish hospitality code in the time of Jesus required that the women of the household provide refreshment and whatever other needs they might anticipate to make their guests comfortable. In addition, women were not included in the normal social setting of male conversation, and certainly not in any spiritual conversation. For example the disciples were astonished that Jesus was speaking with a woman—the Samaritan woman at the well (John 4:27). Some other examples come from William E. Phipps, author of *Assertive Biblical Women,* who quotes an ancient Rabbi who wrote in *The Mishnah,* warning that "He who talks much with women brings evil upon himself and neglects the study of Torah and in the end will go to hell." Another rabbi wrote in *The Jerusalem Talmud,* admonishing men to "Let the words of the Torah burn up but let them not be transmitted to a woman."

Women were forbidden to touch the Torah or to be taught what it said. Phipps says that it was more than violating social mores when a woman sought to learn. Even in the Synagogues women were kept out of sight in another area that was not set aside for the exclusive male worship of Jehovah (Exodus 38:8).

Such restrictive attitudes may seem like ancient concepts, but they parallel the master-slave relationships of the last century when it was illegal to teach a slave to read or write. Phipps writes that, "Likewise, those who loathed uppity women realized that, without literacy and intellectual training, they would be more tractable and deferential." It should be noted, however, that these were men's rules, not God's laws.

In fact, through Moses—at least once in a while—women were commanded to hear the written laws of

God so that they could learn them and do what God instructed.

> *Moses commanded them: "Every seventh year, in the scheduled year of remission, during the festival of booths, when all Israel comes to appear before the LORD your God at the place that he will choose, you shall read this law before all Israel in their hearing. Assemble the people —men, women, and children, as well as the aliens residing in your towns —so that they may hear and learn to fear the LORD your God and to observe diligently all the words of this law, and so that their children, who have not known it, may hear and learn to fear the LORD your God, as long as you live in the land that you are crossing over the Jordan to possess."*
>
> Deuteronomy 31:10-13

The record of Luke, about the day that Mary sat at the feet of Jesus, suggests that Jesus was talking about spiritual matters. Jesus alludes to the spiritual when he suggests to Martha that Mary has chosen something better than meal preparation and hostessing. He said that what Mary was getting could not be taken away from her. In that case, if she was listening and learning about spiritual matters, Mary truly crossed over a well establish line. Perhaps the implied violation of that customary taboo of women learning spirituality is why Martha was trying to get her sister Mary back into line in the kitchen where women were thought to belong. However, in light of the historical traditions associated with Martha after Jesus corrected her that day, and as recorded by tradition after the resurrection of Jesus, it is likely that Martha learned from Jesus in this incident how to align her priorities with spiritual matters modeled by the Messiah.

As one sign of his acceptance of Martha and her behavior, Jesus returned often to be served by her. We can glimpse her serving at a dinner party for Jesus, just six days before his final Passover. No mention is made of sisterly conflict or negative comment when Martha is serving and Mary interrupts the festivities to sit again at the feet of Jesus, using her hair to wipe his feet with her costly perfume. Jesus accepts Martha's service to him, without any additional comments, even when Mary bestows her gift and attention. Jesus does not say that Martha should anoint him as Mary did. But when Mary is attacked by Judas for her generosity, Jesus defends Mary's right to express herself and her care and concern for him in her own way—presumably just as Martha was expressing herself and her care and concern for him in her own way, by serving the meal.

From all accounts, Jesus never discouraged women from expressing themselves with him. Nor did Jesus discourage women from approaching him or just being in his presence. In fact, Jesus included women in his entourage. Among the many women who came up to Jerusalem with Jesus, those women named included Mary Magdalene, and Mary the mother of James the younger and of Joses, and Salome (Mark 15:40-41). After Jesus healed Mary Magdalene from seven demons, cured Joanna, the wife of Herod's steward Chuza, and Susanna, as well as many other women, he taught them, traveled with them, and accepted support from them, financially and physically (Mark 15:41; Luke 8:1-3).

Even when a stranger came from behind him in the crowd and touched the hem of his garment, he did not rebuke the woman, but acknowledged her great faith and pronounced her well (Matthew (:22; Mark 5:34; Luke 8:47-48). Another time, when the disciples told him to send away a woman who shouted after Jesus to heal her daughter, instead of sending her away, he stopped and talked with the woman—granting her request (Matthew 15:28; Mark 7:29).

When the scribes and Pharisees were trying to get Jesus to condemn a woman caught in the act of adultery, Jesus refused to condemn her. Instead, he told them that the person without sin could throw the first stone at her. Then he bent down and wrote on the ground. He may have been writing a list of names and corresponding sins. Otherwise, why would the crowd leave, one by one, beginning with the elders?

It is interesting to note the number of times the Bible records Jesus defending the words and actions of women with whom he came into contact. Jesus openly discounted the tradition of ignoring, using, and mistreating women. Jesus, the rebel, astonished everyone by the way he welcomed women who were sick, women who were unclean, women who were foreign, or women who rebelled against their traditional roles. When such women indicated their desires or even pressed him for favors, he granted their requests for healings, deliverances, forgiveness, and resurrections. Martha and Mary are both women who received such egalitarian treatment from Jesus. And that same egalitarian Jesus of Nazareth is the same Jesus Christ from yesterday, her in our present today, and with us forever (Hebrews 13:8).

Martha Facts, Legends, & Concepts

• "Only in this reference to Martha in Luke 10:40 has the Greek word been interpreted by the writers of Greek lexicons (dictionaries) as referring to domestic duties," writes Margaret Wold, author of *Women of Faith and Spirit*. Continuing, she points out that John "views Martha in the role of 'server' (again the same word as the one used for the service of deacons and ministers) at a supper given for Jesus and his disciples (John 12:2)." Wold states that Martha "was assuming a role not given to women in the orthodox Jewish community. Women were not permitted to be present at male gatherings." Martha may have been functioning as a forerunner of deacons (Acts 6).

• An ancient apocryphal gospel records Martha and Mary among those who were present at the crucifixion of Christ.

• It is also believed that Martha and Mary were among those women who went to the tomb early in the morning in order to anoint the dead body of Jesus with the customary burial spices.

• Legend says that Martha, Mary, and Lazarus were banished from Palestine with other Christians. The unbelievers set them adrift on a raft without a rudder to send them to their death. But instead of perishing at sea, the three landed in France and each continued to have fruitful ministries.

• In 1431, Lucas Moser painted "Martha, Lazarus and Maximinus after landing at Marseilles", now at the Magdalene Alter at Tiefenbronn. A pictorial story of their journey remains on the altar at Tiefenbronn. After their landing in France the three from Bethany became involved in missionary work, with Lazarus becoming a bishop.

• The Martha tradition says that she led an ascetic life. Martha become a vegetarian and directed a convent. Her life was devoted to spiritual matters and she preached, healed the sick, and even raised someone from the dead who had wanted to hear her preach.

• An ancient legend says that Martha overcame a dragon named Tarascus, a half-animal and half-fish who was reported to be bigger than an ox and longer than a horse. This dragon had teeth like swords which were pointed like horns. The dragon was symbolic of the old order, evil, and what was demonic. Martha conquered the dragon and saved the people who sought her help.

• Tradition says that Martha met her death by drowning as she swam across a river.

• One of many paintings of Martha from the Middle Ages (1517) showing "Martha Defeating the Dragon" is in Nuremberg at the Church of St. Laurence.

• While Martha came along on the coattails of her brother Lazarus and as a secondary figure to her more popular sister Mary, in the south of France, Martha was the object of veneration for herself alone by the tenth century.

• In the eleventh century in Tarascon a church was named for Martha, and it claimed that her relics were there.

- At the Pilgrimage Church of Madonna d'Ongero in Carona, near Lugano, Martha appears in an early eighteenth century sculpture, with a cross in one hand and what appears to be a tethered dragon subdued at her feet.

- From the twelfth century through the end of the Middle Ages, Martha was taken as the role model and often the name of women's religious and social groups and organizations who were rebelling against the hierarchical orders in church and society.

- Martha was made the patron saint of churches and communities specializing in care for the plague sufferers, such as the Humiliati, the Franciscans, and the Compagnia della Morte.

- An order of monks dedicated to care for victims of the plague built a Martha church above Lugano. It remains in a half-ruined state today. Inside, Martha is pictured in Gothic frescoes as a white clothed guardian nurse, consecrating the kneeling brothers of the order to their service to the suffering.

- Around 1300, a mystic and Dominican monk named Meister Eckhart preached the Martha and Mary story in Luke to contrast the wise, prepared virgin Martha with the pleasure-seeking, self-absorbed woman, Mary.

- In 1336, in a chapel in the Church of Santa Croce in Florence, Giovanni di Milano portrayed Martha as the host at Bethany and illuminated her with an inner light.

- Dominican preachers painted Martha. One was Fra

Angelico who painted "The Prayer of Jesus in the Garden of Gethsemane" in the Monastery of San Marco in Florence. In its foreground are Martha and Mary who are identified by their names in their haloes. They are awake as Peter, James, and John sleep. While the disciples recline, Martha and Mary sit, but Mary's head is bowed while she reads a book. On the other hand, Martha remains erect, with eyes alert and hands steepled in prayer, keeping watch as Jesus prays.

- Dominicans named hospitals and homes for widows after Martha, erecting her statue in them.

- Martha is pictured in Jacob Acker's fifteenth century painting, alongside Mary Magdalene at the Magdalene altar of Tiefenbronn. (For some time Mary Magdalene was incorrectly thought to be Mary of Bethany.)

- Ignatius Loyola, founder of the Jesuit order (in 1534), is reported to have held Martha in special veneration.

- Nuremberg is home of a pilgrim's hospital which had a small mediaeval Martha church associating her as a patron saint concerned with activism.

- Martha has been immortalized through art by Berhardino Luini, Antonio Corregio, and Bartholomew Zeitblom.

- "...her [Mary] usual role was to take her place beside her sister in the preparation and serving of food (otherwise her sister would not have complained that Mary had 'left' her to serve alone)..." justifies Margaret Wold, author of *Women of Faith and Spirit*.

Mary Facts, Legends, & Concepts

- "Mary is doing the unprecedented: she sits at the feet of a teacher, a rabbi, in the company of men, and receives his teaching and religious instruction..." writes Janice Nunnally-Cox, author of *Fore-Mothers: Women of the Bible*. She adds, "Mary's actions were a distinct break with Jewish custom. Jesus must have encouraged her . . ."

- Margaret Wold, author of *Women of Faith and Spirit*, writes that "Mary was not only affirmed and supported in her action; she was lifted up as a model for women in the years to come." Wold says that "The rediscovery of Jesus' pledge to Mary has been an enormous encouragement to women who have longed to be part of a community of scholars dedicated to the study of God and God's revelation."

- Paul Tillich writes in a chapter called "Our Ultimate Concern" in his book entitled, *The New Being*, that "Mary is concerned about one thing, which is infinite, ultimate, lasting."

- "Jesus inspires Mary to break out of the cage of conventions and realize that a woman can be something other than a homebody," writes William E. Phipps, in *Assertive Biblical Women*. Phipps continues saying that, "he [Jesus] admires her eagerness for learning and, in effect, her desire to be liberated from the limitations of her gender-defined role."

- Peter Ketter writes in *Christ and Womankind* that "Every housewife should follow Mary's example and for a while free herself to be open to new spiritual impulses."

- On the other hand, Meister Eckhart, author of *Ewige Geburt* writes that "We suspect that dear Mary sits there more out of pleasure than for her spiritual advancement." Eckhart says, "That is why Martha says, 'Lord, make her get up!', because she is afraid that Mary might continue in this delight and not advance in any way."

- Rudolf Bultmann, author of the book entitled, *The Gospel of John,* writes that "In Mary, then, we find a portrayal of the first stage of faith, beyond which her sister had advanced . . . Mary does not have Martha's certainty."

- Elisabeth Moltmann-Wendel writes in *The Women Around Jesus* that (Referring to the frequent but inaccurate confusion between Mary of Bethany and Mary of Magdala.):

> Mary of Bethany suffers the fate of many women: her voice is not loud, what she says is not original, her story is not dramatic. Her behaviour is not noticeable, her conduct is modest. She seems sympathetic, but by the next time people have forgotten her name and confuse her with another woman who has made more of an impression.

- Edith Deen, author of *All of the Women of the Bible,* writes that "Mary was following the custom of this time, that of refreshing guests at banquets by pouring cool and fragrant ointments on their heads and sometimes their feet."

- "The Word of God, faith and deeds belonged together, inseparably. Mary felt this in the depths of her soul. She felt a stirring desire to do something," Glen Karssen writes, in *Her Name Is Woman*. "She wanted to express her thankfulness to her Lord, perhaps for the last time . . . Her decision was made," Karssen continues, " The perfume was very costly. The amount in the jar represented a laborer's wages for an entire year . . . It was time to do something for him now."

- Mary of Bethany was one of the women who anointed Jesus. The first woman to anoint Jesus is unnamed, and referred to as a sinner in Luke 7:36-50. The time of her anointing was early in the ministry of Jesus, probably prior to the death of John the Baptist. In addition, the anointing took place in the city, at the house of Simon the Pharisee (Luke 7:37, 40). While she also bathed the feet of Jesus with her tears and dried them with her hair, her act was not an anointing for burial which would be told in remembrance of her as was Mary's anointing. Instead, after Jesus taught Simon and the crowd a lesson in love and forgiveness, the unnamed sinner was forgiven and sent on her way.

- Mary's act of anointing had a history dating back to Egyptian days before the Israelites entered the wilderness. Originally, anointing was a religious ritual reserved for the transfer of "holiness and virtue of the deity in whose name the rite was performed, as well as a special spiritual endowment" upon the king, according to The Family Bible Encyclopedia. In addition, olive oil, often mixed with perfume, was used as a cleansing agent on exposed parts of the body to lessen the effects of extreme heat and high lime content of the dust around Palestine, as a way to honor a guest.

Reflection

Some women identify more with one sister or the other. For a longer period of time, Mary has enjoyed the positive reputation of being the spiritual sister, concerned with the Heavenly and Divine. On the other hand, Martha has endured the negative reputation of being overly concerned with the concerns of everyday life. In *Her Name Is Woman,* author Glen Karssen, demonstrates the promotion of the negative concept of being a "Martha" type. In the author's own words:

> Martha suffered from self-pity . . . Martha didn't seem to care that she was accusing her sister in the presence of her guests and that she was implicating Jesus in the accusation! And that was not all. She dared to order the Master to make Mary come and help her.

This is one popular interpretation of the Luke account which introduces us to Martha and Mary of Bethany. The words are on the pages of the Bible, but the tone and inflection of voice and body language are invisible. When we reread the passage in a softer, questioning tone, we see another picture. (Below, possible behaviors and attitudes are [bracketed].)

> Luke 10:38-42 *Now as they went on their way, he entered a certain village, where a woman named Martha welcomed him into her home* [Martha was eager to entertain and please her guest, Jesus]. *She had a sister named Mary, who* [usually helped her but unlike her usual self, that day she] *sat at the Lord's feet and listened to what he was*

saying. But Martha [who also wanted to be in on the social and spiritual conversation] *was distracted by her many tasks* [because she realized that Jesus was no ordinary guest and everything should be extraordinary for him]; *so she came to him* [waiting politely for him to acknowledge her and signal her to speak] *and asked* [in a soft, gentle tone, with the pitch rising questioningly on the last word], *"Lord, do you not care that my sister has left me to do all the work by myself?* [Jesus smiled at her assuredly and nodded "yes" to which Martha replied] *Tell her then to help me." But the Lord* [smiled at Martha and] *answered her* [in the same soft, gentle tone that Martha had used to speak to him], *"Martha, Martha, you are worried and distracted by many things; there is need of only one thing. Mary has chosen the better part* [gesturing to Martha to sit at his feet next to Mary], *which will not be taken away from her* [Mary smiled at Martha, moved over to make room for her, and extended her hand to invite Martha to sit down with her at the feet of Jesus]."

The forgoing scenario or any number of other variations is quite possible. Remembering the tradition of the times being the quiet subjection and servility of women, why then does Martha almost always get such a hard, negative reading? It has been suggested by Elisabeth Moltmann-Wendel, author of *The Women Around Jesus,* that it was a century later when the active, administrative Martha was devalued (in order to give men the active administrative roles in the church), and the contemplative, comforting, submissive attitude of Mary was exalted (in order to relegate women to the nonverbal, nonleadership roles in the church).

Yes, it appears that Martha was a woman of action, and Mary a woman of repose. For example, examine the behavior of each sister after the death of Lazarus. Martha went out to meet Jesus, not like her sister Mary who sat at home in the comfort of consoling mourners. Martha did not cry, as Mary did. Martha stood face-to-face with Jesus, not falling at his feet as Mary did. Martha was assertive, verbally making her thoughts, feelings, and requests known to Jesus. Mary was submissive and laid her thoughts and feelings at the feet of Jesus with tears—too timid to make any request. Martha assertively went toe-to-toe with Jesus by asking for answers, while Mary toed the line of a non-questioning female. Martha wanted her brother back and got right to the issue at hand, not giving up as Mary did. Martha appeared confident, and Mary appeared helpless. Martha was stubborn, and Mary was yielding.

Each sister had a different style, personality, and goal. Both are valuable role models for all of us. Mary demonstrated qualities of character which are often thought of as silently powerful. Martha demonstrated qualities of character which are verbally powerful.

For examples: Martha was successful in verbally wrestling with the Lord for her brother's life, just as Jacob wrestled with the Lord physically at Peniel (Genesis 32:22-32). Martha acknowledged Jesus as the Messiah and further acknowledged his power with God to get whatever he asked. Martha asked and she received her brother raised from the dead.

It is important to note that at the time of the death

of Lazarus it had become spiritually and physically dangerous for the Jewish people to associate with Jesus. One example is found in John 9:22: *"His parents said this because they were afraid of the Jews; for the Jews had already agreed that anyone who confessed Jesus to be the Messiah would be put out of the synagogue."* Yet, Martha, before all the Jerusalem Jews, openly made her confession of faith in Jesus as The Christ in John 11:27: *"She said to him, 'Yes, Lord, I believe that you are the Messiah, the Son of God, the one coming into the world.'"*

This confession of Jesus as The Christ was only uttered on one other occasion in the other Gospels, by Peter (Matthew 16:15, Mark 8:29, Luke 9:20). His confession marked him as an apostle, and the church was built upon Peter's confession. Catholic Popes believe that they are Peter's successors. However, going one step beyond Peter's confession, Martha, even though—or because—she stepped beyond her traditional feminine role, was the first to experience resurrection.

Yet, in time Martha became the patron saint of housewives and cooks. Martha's saint's day is July 29. In the Catholic tradition, Martha is relegated to the domestic, housekeeper order—which is necessary and has God's approval, but will never attain the high rank of spirituality. For instance, an order of lay brothers dedicated to care for victims of the plague built a Martha church above Lugano. It remains in a half-ruined state today. Inside, Martha is pictured as a white clothed guardian nurse, consecrating the kneeling brothers of the order to their service to the suffering. Also, Nuremberg is the home of a pilgrim's hospital with a small mediaeval Martha church which associated her as a patron saint concerned with activism.

In short, Martha satisfies the need for a good wife and mother. Good in this sense means that she is busy about the activities that help us feel properly "mothered". Of course, such actions are often correlated to the concept of "righteousness by works" rather than the concept of being inactive and receiving acceptance by grace.

However, Bultmann believes that Martha's faith is stronger than Mary's. In addition, Elisabeth Moltmann-Wendel, author of *The Women Around Jesus,* comments on Leipoldt's assertion that "'Mary feels it much more deeply than Martha.'" She immediately writes:

> But is not this a presupposition, a prejudiced view of what a woman and her faith should be: obedient, recognizing the limitations, asking nothing more, doubting nothing, falling into line? John, though, wanted to portray quite a different woman: the rebel, who does not toe the line, who will not be satisfied with what a man says to her.

Was Martha a woman of great faith which caused her to act or a woman of action who moved into great faith? If Moltmann-Wendel's perception of a strong Martha of faith is accurate, then how did Martha's positive, active, faith role model and reputation suffer rebuke and dismissal over the years? Perhaps she suffered from a similar prejudice which today's strong, assertive, confronting woman faces. Martha may have made her contemporaries too uncomfortable! Opponents of female competence and emancipation promote the concept that such women are dangerous and that modesty and restraint, clearly seen in the examples written of Mary, are attributes of woman which our society continues to prefer supporting. But they are not attributes which John records as being able to transcend death and bring life to our brothers. John's Martha deserves another chance to stand tall and believe that whatever she asks of the Lord, God will do—and so can we, sisters and brothers!

Wichern wrote that "Martha must be a Mary and the true Mary must also be a Martha; both are sisters." Joyce Hollyday, author of *Clothed with the Sun*, writes that Jesus:

> ...refused to corner these women into prescribed roles, acknowledging that there is need for both vigorous caregiving and quiet listening. He made clear that there is room in the faith for the servant activist as well as the contemplative.

Taking note of the reactions of Jesus toward these sisters with very different temperaments, gifts, and expectations, we should consider giving our hearts, hands, and heads to lead, learn, and listen while we accept, appreciate, and applaud our sisters. Whatever their choices have been, are, or will be, we can be there to affirm their efforts and sincerity—whether cooking or contemplating—in this, their journey called life. And as we chose to move toward, between, or within temperaments, gifts, and expectations, we can also be grateful that Jesus has given us the example and ability to graciously accept the diversity of our sisters and brothers—as well as ourselves.

Martha
Luke 10:38, 40-41; John 11:1, 5, 19-21, 24, 30, 39;12:2

Martha of Bethany invited Jesus into her home. Jesus became the friend of Martha, regardless of or because of Jesus correcting Martha's attitude about the importance of spiritual matters versus domestic matters. Martha entertained Jesus and his disciples on many occasions, serving them meals as well as hospitality. When her brother became very ill, Martha and her sister sent for Jesus. Jesus delayed and Lazarus died. When Martha confronted Jesus as a friend, he was direct with her also—and Lazarus was raised from the dead.

Focus Virtue: Friendliness

One who forgives an affront fosters friendship, but one who dwells on disputes will alienate a friend.

Proverbs 17:9

Martha displayed her friendliness by inviting Jesus into her home. In her eagerness to show her friendliness through her domestic skills, Martha could have heard an affront in the words of Jesus, *"Martha, Martha, you are worried and distracted by many things; there is need of only one thing. Mary has chosen the better part, which will not be taken away from her"* (Luke 10:42). But the friendly act of taking an interest in another person allowed Martha to receive the words of Jesus. When we are friendly to someone, we hear things differently and we say things differently—with warmth and concern.

Friendliness will be in my heart to be interested, in my mind to be courteous, on my face to show warmth, on my lips to say kindness, and in my hands to do good things.

Martha & Mary

Mary
Luke 10:39-42; John 11:1-2, 19-20, 28, 31-31, 45; 12:3

Mary of Bethany sat at the feet of Jesus, listening to him as her sister prepared for the guests. When Mary was criticized for not helping, Jesus defended her desire to be present in spiritual matters, rather than domestic matters. The week before the crucifixion of Jesus, Mary anointed the feet of Jesus with costly perfume, and wiped them with her hair. When Judas criticized her for the financial waste, Jesus defended Mary and proclaimed that her deed of preparation for his burial would be told in remembrance of her, forever.

Focus Virtue: Reverence

Therefore, since we are receiving a kingdom that cannot be shaken, let us give thanks, by which we offer to God an acceptable worship with reverence and awe;

Hebrews 12:28

Mary: sat at the feet of Jesus, listening attentively and reverently; knelt at the feet of Jesus, submitting respectfully and reverently; wiped the feet of Jesus, serving tenderly and reverently. The deep respect and special care that Mary showed for Jesus is reverence. We can show reverence for the things in our material world as well as for the things in our spiritual world. Reverence is an attitude as well as a practice. Listening, reflecting, and praying during times of stillness can be the beginning of reverence. We can help others develop reverence by our attitude of deep respect for what is sacred to us, to others, and to God.

Everyday I will take time to value the sacred and experience reverence.

Virtues Reflection: Martha & Mary

We know that Martha and Mary are included in the scriptures for several of reasons—as are their other biblical sisters. Some of the biblical Virtues that these sisters model for us are trust, faith, and hope, all to be admired and emulated. In addition, these biblical sisters also demonstrate the need to develop and exercise some of their other Virtues, just as we all may need to do.

When you read, consider, and discuss the stories of these sisters, Martha and Mary, understand the Virtues each of them are modeling. *(See the Focus Virtues list in Chapter One.)* Make time to identify the developed Virtues of Martha and the developed Virtues of Mary. Then complete the following exercise with Martha and Mary in mind.

Which one of the developed Virtues of Martha do you most appreciate, today?

Which one of the developed Virtues of Mary do you most appreciate, today?

How have these Virtues been part of your life in the past or in the present?

How do you see these Virtues or the need for them in your life, now?

What can you do to further develop these Virtues in your life?

In what ways has this study helped you?

Action Scripture

James 2:14-18 *What good is it, my brothers and sisters, if you say you have faith but do not have works? Can faith save you? If a brother or sister is naked and lacks daily food, and one of you says to them, "Go in peace; keep warm and eat your fill," and yet you do not supply their bodily needs, what is the good of that? So faith by itself, if it has no works, is dead. But someone will say, "You have faith and I have works." Show me your faith apart from your works, and I by my works will show you my faith.*

Grateful Prayer

Gracious God, it is You who have made us, forming us from our mother's womb with all Your goodness within us. Therefore, we ask to feel Your goodness within us, now. Let Your goodness spring up within us and flow from us to one another, with love. As Your Spirit guides us into all truth, we pray to see clearly our choices for good and respond to You with reverence. Strengthen us with courage to do the good that we can each day. Bless us in all we do, so that we may bless others, as well as You. AMEN

Chapter Six

Bernice & Drusilla

*Being born a female is only the
beginning of sisterhood.*
Christine M. Carpenter

Bernice & Drusilla

> **Acts 24:22-27** But Felix, who was rather well informed about the Way, adjourned the hearing with the comment, "When Lysias the tribune comes down, I will decide your case." Then he ordered the centurion to keep him in custody, but to let him have some liberty and not to prevent any of his friends from taking care of his needs. Some days later when Felix came with his wife Drusilla, who was Jewish, he sent for Paul and heard him speak concerning faith in Christ Jesus. And as he discussed justice, self-control, and the coming judgment, Felix became frightened and said, "Go away for the present; when I have an opportunity, I will send for you." At the same time he hoped that money would be given him by Paul, and for that reason he used to send for him very often and converse with him. After two years had passed, Felix was succeeded by Porcius Festus; and since he wanted to grant the Jews a favor, Felix left Paul in prison.

Since Drusilla was a Jewess, what reaction do you think she had to Paul's message of Jesus as the Jewish Messiah?

a. She accepted and secretly believed.

b. She believed and shared Jesus with everyone.

c. She was skeptical, but interested.

d. She did not believe a word and asked her husband, Felix, to make sure Paul would not be able to make trouble for the Jews, anymore.

e. Other?

How did Drusilla become a Jew?

a. Her mother was a Jew.

b. She was converted.

c. She married a Jew.

d. She bought the right, just as non Romans could buy Roman citizenship.

e. Other?

> **Acts 25:1-3** Three days after Festus had arrived in the province, he went up from Caesarea to Jerusalem where the chief priests and the leaders of the Jews gave him a report against Paul. They appealed to him and requested, as a favor to them against Paul, to have him transferred to Jerusalem. They were, in fact, planning an ambush to kill him along the way.
> **Acts 25:7-10a** When he arrived, the Jews who had gone down from Jerusalem surrounded him, bringing many serious charges against him, which they could not prove. Paul said in his defense, "I have in no way committed an offense against the law of the Jews, or against the temple, or against the emperor." But Festus, wishing to do the Jews a favor, asked Paul, "Do you wish to go up to Jerusalem and be tried there before me on these charges?" Paul said, "I am appealing to the emperor's tribunal; this is where I should be tried."

In the two years Felix ruled, how often do you think he and his wife, Drusilla, heard and/or discussed Paul's defense with each other? With Festus?

Why is Drusilla mentioned only once (Acts 24:24) in the Bible?

a. She was a witness to Paul's repeated defense and gave Luke, the writer of Acts, these details.

b. She was one of the people who could have gotten Paul released from prison and did not.

c. Someone told Luke that she was present, so he recorded her name.

d. She believed Paul's message and accepted Christ as her Messiah and became a reliable witness to the facts recorded by Luke in this Acts passage.

e. Other?

What do you think Paul said the times Drusilla heard him?

> **Excerpts from Acts 25:13-22** After several days had passed, King Agrippa and Bernice arrived at Caesarea to welcome Festus... [and] Festus laid Paul's case before the king, saying, "There is a man here who was left in prison by Felix. When I was in Jerusalem, the chief priests and the elders of the Jews informed me about him and asked for a sentence against him....So when they met here, I lost no time, but on the next day took my seat on the tribunal and ordered the man to be brought. When the accusers stood up, they did not charge him with any of the crimes that I was expecting. Instead they had certain points of disagreement with him about their own religion and about a certain Jesus, who had died, but whom Paul asserted to be alive.... I ordered him to be held until I could send him to the emperor." Agrippa said to Festus, "I would like to hear the man myself." "Tomorrow," he said, "you will hear him."

Why is Bernice mentioned by name as accompanying King Agrippa?

a. She was known to be interested in matters pertaining to the Jews and was a reliable witness others could question about this incident.
b. Luke, the author of Acts included every detail he could, and Bernice was reported as being present at the proceedings.
c. Bernice was one of the few women who were known to openly state that Paul had done nothing worthy of death and could be set free, had he not appealed to the Emperor.
d. Other?

What religion do you think Drusilla's sister, Bernice, practiced?

What religion was King Agrippa II?

> **Acts 25:23-26:3** So on the next day Agrippa and Bernice came with great pomp, and they entered the audience hall with the military tribunes and the prominent men of the city. Then Festus gave the order and Paul was brought in. And Festus said, "King Agrippa... Therefore I have brought him before all of you, and especially before you, King Agrippa, so that, after we have examined him, I may have something to write — for it seems to me unreasonable to send a prisoner without indicating the charges against him." Agrippa said to Paul, "You have permission to speak for yourself." Then Paul stretched out his hand and began to defend himself: "I consider myself fortunate that it is before you, King Agrippa, I am to make my defense today against all the accusations of the Jews, because you are especially familiar with all the customs and controversies of the Jews; therefore I beg of you to listen to me patiently . . ."

Describe the pomp and circumstance with which Agrippa and Bernice may have entered the court to hear Paul.

Music: Head dress:

Costume: Jewelry:

Attendants: Other:

What do you think Drusilla had already told Bernice about Paul and/or his testimony of Jesus as the Christ, the Jewish Messiah?

What do you think Bernice expected Paul to say?

Would you like to have been there that day?

Why?

> **Acts 26:19-26** "After that, King Agrippa, I was not disobedient to the heavenly vision, but declared first to those in Damascus, then in Jerusalem and throughout the countryside of Judea, and also to the Gentiles, that they should repent and turn to God and do deeds consistent with repentance. For this reason the Jews seized me in the temple and tried to kill me. To this day I have had help from God, and so I stand here, testifying to both small and great, saying nothing but what the prophets and Moses said would take place: that the Messiah must suffer, and that, by being the first to rise from the dead, he would proclaim light both to our people and to the Gentiles." While he was making this defense, Festus exclaimed, "You are out of your mind, Paul! Too much learning is driving you insane!" But Paul said, "I am not out of my mind, most excellent Festus, but I am speaking the sober truth. Indeed the king knows about these things, and to him I speak freely; for I am certain that none of these things has escaped his notice, for this was not done in a corner. "

Why do you think Bernice came and stayed to hear Paul?

a. Her sister had recommended him as an interesting religious speaker.

b. Her brother, Agrippa II, would not go anywhere without her.

c. She wanted to know more about Paul's Jesus.

d. She already knew the message of Paul and wanted to lend him support in court.

e. Other?

What do you think Bernice was thinking about Paul's message so far?

What do you think about the message of Paul so far?

> **Acts 26:27-32** "King Agrippa, do you believe the prophets? I know that you believe." Agrippa said to Paul, "Are you so quickly persuading me to become a Christian?" Paul replied, "Whether quickly or not, I pray to God that not only you but also all who are listening to me today might become such as I am—except for these chains." Then the king got up, and with him the governor and Bernice and those who had been seated with them; and as they were leaving, they said to one another, "This man is doing nothing to deserve death or imprisonment." Agrippa said to Festus, "This man could have been set free if he had not appealed to the emperor."

How do you think Bernice was affected by Paul's speech?

a. She left the company of her brother, permanently, in order to avoid any appearance of evil.

b. She committed herself to Paul's message of Christ and became an advocate of justice for all.

c. She left her life in the Royal Court and lived among the Jews as a peasant, serving Christ.

d. She thought it was a good message, but never made a commitment to Christ.

e. She was totally unaffected and after that day she did not think twice about Paul or the Christ that he preached at his defense.

e. Other?

Share a time when someone talked to you about Christ's redemption.

Share a time when you talked with a sister or other person about Christ's redemption.

As a result of hearing Paul's message, what might you do or say to someone?

Bernice & Drusilla's Family Tree

King Herod the Great*

- Antipas^ [A half-brother of Philip]
- Aristobulus [By Wife #1 whom King Herod loved]
- Philip [Half brother of Antipas]
- Unnamed In Scripture

Aristobulus — Herodias

Herodias — Salome [By Herodias' first husband, Philip]

Herodias — Herod of Chalcis#

Unnamed In Scripture — Agrippa I+

Agrippa I+ children: *Bernice'*, *Drusilla"*, **Agrippa II+**

Drusilla" = son [By second husband, Felix]

Legend:
— Blood relatives
- - - Marriage partners

*Bernice and Drusilla were great-granddaughters of King Herod the Great. After Jesus was born in Bethlehem of Judea, King Herod ordered the death of all Hebrew babies two years old and younger (Matthew, Chapter 2). King Herod had ten wives.

^ Bernice and Drusilla were great-nieces of Herod Antipas, tetrarch of Galilee. Herod Antipas had John the Baptist beheaded, at the bidding of his wife, Herodias, through her daughter Salome. Herod Antipas saw Jesus on the eve of the crucifixion. Earlier, Jesus compared him to a "fox" (Luke 13:32).

+ Bernice and Drusilla were daughters of Herod Agrippa I, King of Judea from 37-44, who is known as the first royal prosecutor of the Church.

Herod of Chalcis was the uncle of Bernice and her first husband. She remained with him until he died.

' Tradition says that upon the death of her husband, Herod of Chalcis, Bernice became the constant companion of her brother, Agrippa II. This lent itself to the incestuous gossip about her. She later married King Ptolemy of Sicily, but left him after a few years and rejoined her brother.

" Tradition says that Drusilla was married at fourteen to King Aziz of Emesa. Felix hired a Cypriote magician Atomus to woo Drusilla away from her husband, and so she married Felix. She was about seventeen years old when she was with her husband, Felix, as mentioned in Acts.

+Bernice and Drusilla were sisters of King Agrippa II, King of Judea from 53-100.

= Tradition says that Drusilla and her son by Felix were killed by lava in the eruption of Vesuvius that destroyed Pompeii.

The Roman Court System

The Romans are famous for their legal institutions and evidence shows that they had established a proper and uniform system of law courts throughout the provinces of the Roman Empire. These courts were open to all inhabitants of the land—Roman, Jew, or otherwise. One example of the openness of the court system is found in the recounting of the time Paul's preaching stirred up the people of Ephesus. It was the town clerk who appeased the people by pointing out that they could take any grievance to the courts where the deputies could handle the matter peaceably.

> *But when the town clerk had quieted the crowd, he said, "Citizens of Ephesus, who is there that does not know that the city of the Ephesians is the temple keeper of the great Artemis and of the statue that fell from heaven? Since these things cannot be denied, you ought to be quiet and do nothing rash. You have brought these men here who are neither temple robbers nor blasphemers of our goddess. If therefore Demetrius and the artisans with him have a complaint against anyone, the courts are open, and there are proconsuls; let them bring charges there against one another. If there is anything further you want to know, it must be settled in the regular assembly.*
>
> Acts 19:35-39

Some general points about the Roman court system include the summoning of the plaintiff's opponent to appear in court. If the defendant refused to appear in court, the plaintiff could ask any bystander to witness the defendant's receipt of the court summons and its refusal. The ritual for this procedure involved the plaintiff touching the ear of the witness to symbolize that he was making him listen to the terms of the summons. If the defendant wanted to, the matter could be settled at once out of court by satisfying the plaintiff's requirements as stated in the summons. Should the defendant not comply and refuse to agree to come peaceably to court, then the plaintiff was allowed to use force with the defendant.

In the case of sickness or the elderly, the plaintiff was required to provide the defendant with transportation. However, the transportation did not need to be luxurious. For example, it was not required that the car or litter have cushions.

Once the matter was to go before the court, the defendant could secure an advocate to appear for the defendant if the defendant did not want to represent himself. Advocates, similar to our lawyers, were paid on what we call a sliding scale, according to the defendant's income. If no one appeared on the set day and time, in person, to represent the plaintiff or the defendant, the side present won the lawsuit.

When the dispute was over property, either the whole piece of property or some part representing the property had to be presented in court. For example, if the ownership of a flock of sheep was in dispute, then one sheep or a lock of wool had to be entered into court as we would enter an exhibit in our process, today. Other examples include disputes over a house requiring a brick to be presented in court, or in the case of a dispute over a ship, then a piece of the ship's timber or some other piece of the ship would have to be presented in court.

At the first hearing the praetor could make an immediate decision to be accepted by the parties involved. When sunset came, any unsettled case was set for a later appearance and both parties were required to provide bail. However, if at any time the praetor's decision was not accepted, the parties were required to make bail and their case was sent to a judge to be tried. A trial in front of a judge could take place within two days or postponed until a later date. A postponement was made when additional evidence was needed to be gathered or a principle party was needed in court and had to travel a distance or recover from an illness.

In the case of civil suits, actions *in rem* were to establish property rights or privileges of some type. Actions *in personam* were to settle injurious acts or torts, including breach of contract. All actions were initially heard by a praetor, then a judge if necessary. In the case of Paul, he appealed to our version of the Supreme Court, the Emperor. Sometime after the first century, local governors made the decisions on all cases in their jurisdiction.

In addition to hearing and rendering verdicts in cases, both the praetor and judge were always open to the idea of receiving gifts and financial considerations from those appearing before them in court. Today, in the United States of America we would think that this would be a bribe and illegal. However, giving officials gifts was the honorary custom of the day, and still is the custom in some countries. Again, in Paul's case, Felix called for Paul often in hope that money would be given to him by Paul (Acts 24:26).

A criminal action was a *crimen*, and was an offence against religion and the gods. In time a *crimen* became an offence against the State, not against a private individual. Robbery and murder were clearly in this category. The penalty for theft was restitution twice or four times the estimated value of the goods which had been stolen.

Murder, because no amount of tangible exchange of goods could make restitution for the offence, required capital punishment. Some punishments also involved the public humiliation of the offender. The practice of naked crucifixion is one example of punishment plus humiliation for the offender. Brutal and painful punishment was often inflicted. For example, flogging a convicted or accused criminal with a cat o' nine tails was done publicly and privately as punishment. Jesus was mistreated similarly by the Roman guard before his crucifixion.

> *So he released Barabbas for them; and after flogging Jesus, he handed him over to be crucified. Then the soldiers of the governor took Jesus into the governor's headquarters, and they gathered the whole cohort around him. They stripped him and put a scarlet robe on him, and after twisting some thorns into a crown, they put it on his head. They put a reed in his right hand and knelt before him and mocked him, saying, "Hail, King of the Jews!" They spat on him, and took the reed and struck him on the head. After mocking him, they stripped him of the robe and put his own clothes on him. Then they led him away to crucify him.*
>
> Matthew 27:26-31
> (Also see: Mark 15:15-20)

Some offenders avoided death, but perhaps would

have preferred it to the living death they were sentenced to act out as slaves. The equivalent of concentration camps, usually in mines, was used for punishment at prolonged penal labor. Sometimes the offender was put in chains—hands, feet and even chains around the neck.

During this brutal time, *furca,* similar to Chinese board punishment or the pillory, was also used. This very common form of punishment involved the offender carrying a forked wooden structure around the neck while working. While wearing it the offender was often flogged. Scourging was also a popular form of punishment. The Jews used a rod, striking the offender thirteen times on each shoulder and on the loins. No one was to be scourged beyond "forty stripes save one." Tradition says that there was a threefold recitation from a certain verse of a Psalm which contained thirteen words. The offender was given a blow with each word, totaling thirty-nine, which is "forty stripes save one."

Exilium was used at the whim of the Emperor to rid himself of anyone who displeased him in any way. Perhaps it was not as physically brutal a hardship, being banished as punishment. However, the separation from family, friends, and possessions was emotional punishment not just for the offender, but for the others in his or her life. They may have lost their provider, their comforter, or their teacher. Banishment could last as long as until death, or even after death if the offender was denied burial in the realm of the Emperor.

Roads & Travel

In early New Testament times traveling conditions were just about the same as they were throughout Europe until the beginning of the nineteenth century when railways and mechanical vehicles were invented. The Romans constructed and maintained very well made roads throughout their Empire. These roads were the ones that Paul traveled on his missionary journeys and between prisons. Bernice travelled them with her brother Agrippa II to tour his domain. Drusilla travelled them with her husband Felix as they moved their household to different job opportunities.

The Roman Empire was established in 27 B.C. by Augustus. At its peak, the Roman Empire included Western and Southern Europe, Britain, Asia Minor, North Africa, and the Eastern Mediterranean islands. Well constructed roads were essential in order to expedite military forces, goods, and services. Roads were the communication highway of their day. These roadways are said to have connected all individual districts and provinces with the Imperial capital, while keeping them separated form one another. Such a plan expedited the spread of Roman culture and increased trade with the capital. This strategy, having Rome as the hub of the wheel and the roads as the spokes linking each town or city to Rome, also brought the newest and best to Rome and from Rome.

Some of the Roman roads survive in tact today. These roads were usually constructed so that they would be raised some height above the normal ground level. They went in a straight line over hill and through valleys, as much as possible. Their three separate layers consisted of first stones mixed with cement, concrete. The second layer was gravel, rough stone, or broken pottery. On the top layer were large stones very carefully placed together to create as smooth a surface as possible for wheeled traffic to maneuver.

In cities there were raised sidewalks next to the roads, protected by kerb-stones and what we would call gutters for liquid runoff. The liquid runoff included rain water, sewage, irrigation runoff, and other waste water. Stepping stones at convenient intervals, with enough space for wheeled traffic to run between, provided pedestrian accessibility and comfort around the frequent pools of water or mud standing beside the roadways.

According to ancient records, manuscript-drawn maps were made for travellers. The maps were copied and could be purchased in local shops. Guidebooks for tourists were also available. Pausanais put together one of the largest guidebooks—two volumes—for people travelling to Greece. Large maps of the new Empire were compiled by several different people, and remain today.

Just because they had good roads, did not mean that they made good time traveling. It is said that Imperial couriers took 63 days going the northern route from Rome to Alexandria. It took them 54 days to get from Rome to Caesarea. Augustus is believed to have been the first to organize a courier service so that he could retain management, but delegate the working positions to his appointees.

Besides the fast trotting horses of Imperial couriers, the roads could have been used by vehicles, such as litters with poles to be carried on the shoulders of men, much like old sedan-chairs in England. In addition, there could have been wheeled carriages of all types. One such vehicle is described in scripture:

> ...*Now there was an Ethiopian eunuch, a court official of the Candace, queen of the Ethiopians, in charge of her entire treasury. He had come to Jerusalem to worship and was returning home; seated in his chariot, he was reading the prophet Isaiah....So Philip ran up to it and heard him reading the prophet Isaiah. He asked, "Do you understand what you are reading?" He replied, "How can I, unless someone guides me?" And he invited Philip to get in and sit beside him.*
>
> Acts 8:27-31

Notice that the eunuch's chariot was large enough for him to be seated, reading. Perhaps it was large enough for him to have a driver. The chariot was also large enough for Philip to be seated with the eunuch.

Other vehicles may have included the gladiator, one person chariots with galloping steeds. Wagons with solid wheels large enough to transport agriculture or other goods behind teams of horses, mules, or other beasts may have filled the roadways to and from Rome. Carts were used for the local or small load transports. Carriages and coaches of various types were also possible vehicles of transportation to and from the Imperial city. Some vehicles had two wheels, others had four or more—with any number of spokes. Some were elegantly decorated and cushioned, others were plain and functional. Some were for hire, others were exclusively for private use. Some came with hired drivers who were subject to regulations, while others had drivers who knew nothing of driving with care and attention.

Reflection

Traditionally, Bernice and Drusilla have been given the distinction of being identified as the most evil sisters of the New Testament era. Are they truly deserving of this distinction? What evidence is there to bestow such a distinction upon these Jewish women? The Bible refers to Drusilla and Bernice only in reference to their participation in the audience of Paul's defense and proclamation of Jesus. Drusilla, together with her husband Felix, specifically on one occasion, heard Paul. At another time, Bernice, along with her brother Agrippa II, listened to Paul's defense and testimony, and agreed that Paul had done nothing wrong and could be released if it were not for his appeal to the Emperor.

Most of what we know about Drusilla and Bernice has been found in the records of Josephus. For example, the Jewish historian Josephus tells us that during the Jewish War, in the spring of AD 66, a barefooted Bernice, with her hair disheveled, went to see Cestius in Jerusalem to complain about Florus' brutal, murderous acts on the Jews. This would have been after hearing Paul's message of Christ as the Jewish Messiah.

But what of the early history of Drusilla and Bernice? We are given to understand that they were the great-granddaughters of King Herod the Great. He lived from approximately 73 to 4 B.C. and was Idumaean (Greek name of Edom) king of Judea from 37 to 4 B.C. After Jesus was born in Bethlehem of Judea, it was King Herod the Great who spoke with the wise men about The Star and then ordered the death of all Hebrew babies from two years old and younger who lived in his region (Matthew, Chapter 2).

In addition, Drusilla and Bernice were nieces of Herod Antipas. His date of birth is unknown and his death is believed to have been around 40 A.D. He was tetrarch (Roman ruler or governor of a province) of Galilee from about 4 B.C. to 39 A.D. It was Herod Antipas who had John the Baptist beheaded. He had foolishly promised the daughter of his wife, Herodias, that she could ask anything of him as payment for pleasing him and his guests with her dance. After her mother prompted her to make the request, the girl— identified by Josephus as Salome— asked for John's head (Matthew 14:8; Mark 6:24). Jesus had compared Herod Antipas to a "fox" (Luke 13:32) and had told the disciples to beware of the yeast of Herod (Mark 8:15). Herod Antipas later received Jesus from Pilate on the eve of the crucifixion of Jesus, but Jesus would not say a word to Herod.

> *When Pilate heard this, he asked whether the man was a Galilean. And when he learned that he was under Herod's jurisdiction, he sent him off to Herod, who was himself in Jerusalem at that time. When Herod saw Jesus, he was very glad, for he had been wanting to see him for a long time, because he had heard about him and was hoping to see him perform some sign. He questioned him at some length, but Jesus gave him no answer. The chief priests and the scribes stood by, vehemently accusing him. Even Herod with his soldiers treated him with contempt and mocked him; then he put an elegant robe on him, and sent him back to Pilate. That same day Herod and Pilate*

> *became friends with each other; before this they had been enemies.*
>
> Luke 23:6-12

Bernice and Drusilla were also the daughters of Herod Agrippa I who is known as the first royal prosecutor of the Church. He is believed to have lived from approximately 10 B.C. to 44 A.D. and ruled Judea from 37 to 44. Herod Agrippa II was his son, and lived from about 27 to 100 A.D. He ruled from 53 to 100 A.D.

Tradition says that Drusilla was married at age fourteen to King Aziz of Emesa. Drusilla is said to have been beautiful. While the young Drusilla had been married to King Aziz, Felix hired a Cypriote magician, Atomus, to woo Drusilla away from her husband. So Drusilla, a Jew, left her first husband to be married to Felix, a Gentile. She was only about seventeen years old when she was with her husband, Felix, as mentioned in Acts. Tradition says that Drusilla and her son by her second husband, Felix, were both killed by lava in the eruption of Mount Vesuvius that destroyed Pompeii.

The accepted tradition regarding Drusilla's older sister, Bernice, says that Herod of Chalcis was the uncle of Bernice and her first husband. She remained with him until he died. In addition, tradition says that upon the death of her husband, Bernice became the constant companion of her brother, Agrippa II. This lent itself to the incestuous gossip about her. She later married King Ptolemy of Sicily, but left him after a few years and rejoined her brother.

With this brief view of their recorded history, what makes these two women the most evil of sisters? An example of how these sisters have acquired their evil reputation may be found in *All the Women of the Bible*. In her book, Edith Deen writes, "Here she sat [Bernice], a woman who evidently had great influence over her brother. Probably one word from her might have freed Paul from prison. But did she speak such a word? No." These words are taken from Deen's chapter on Drusilla and Bernice, subtitled, "Two Evil Sisters Who Helped Condemn Paul." Deen's concluding paragraph on the sisters says that:

> They come into Bible history for one reason alone, because they were present and occupied influential positions at the trials of the courageous and earnest Christian, Paul. Though he introduced them to the regenerating power of Christ, they quickly retreated into the darkness of their own sensual and selfish lives.

The 1950's opinion of Deen has been well learned and passed on to others over the years. Perhaps Deen inherited her own concept of Bernice and Drusilla. In any or all cases, we may want to stop perpetuating the oral tradition of how evil these and other Bible women were, and reexamine the scriptural record. Even Josephus, the Jewish historian, was not writing from personal experience with Bernice and Drusilla. But a good story lives on, and we love hearing the court intrigue—do we not? Today, many people view Bible characters and events through the lens of Cecile B. DeMill. However, what makes a good movie may not be true to the spirit and intent of what was recorded in the scriptures. As in the retelling of any event or dialogue, many tones and inflections are given to Bible stories and characters that are more exciting, inciting, and marketable than their actual words were meant to communicate.

But what about the accusation that Bernice and Drusilla were present at Paul's hearings in order to influence the authorities to release him? By the lack of record indicating their outspoken support for Paul, are we to identify their biblical silence as evil? Then what will we have to say about the Apostle Peter turning down three opportunities to identify himself with Jesus on the night before the crucifixion? Not only did Peter shun any indication of influencing the authorities to release Jesus, but Peter denied knowing Jesus in the presence of servant girls and bystanders (Matthew 26:69-75). Yet, with out asking for forgiveness, Peter became the leader of the Christian church—honored for his previous confession of Jesus as the Christ (Matthew 16:16; Mark 8:29).

In addition, other women associated with power during the times were not influential with the ruling men in their lives. If they were, Herodias would have had John's head long before she had to trick her husband into killing him (Mark 6:19). Also, the wife of Pilate used the then powerful warnings of a dream, but could not dissuade her husband from being involved in condemning a just man, Jesus (Matthew 27:19). So why would we think that in the case of Paul, Drusilla had more influence with her husband Felix or Bernice with her brother Agrippa or Festus the new procurator? It is more than possible that the sisters discussed Paul and his message with one another and with their men and friends.

Perhaps the sisters did influence their men and others on behalf of fair treatment of Paul. We know that compared to the usual treatment of prisoners during that time, Paul enjoyed relative comfort. He had some degree of freedom and his friends were able to care for him. For example, Acts 27:3 says, *"The next day we put in at Sidon; and Julius treated Paul kindly, and allowed him to go to his friends to be cared for."* In addition, Acts 24:22-23 says:

> *But Felix, who was rather well informed about the Way, adjourned the hearing with the comment, "When Lysias the tribune comes down, I will decide your case." Then he ordered the centurion to keep him in custody, but to let him have some liberty and not to prevent any of his friends from taking care of his needs.*

Is it possible that *"Felix who was rather well informed about the Way* (Christianity)*"* (Acts 24:22) was so because his wife, Drusilla, shared her faith with him? Is it possible that King Agrippa II was *"especially familiar with all the customs and controversies of the Jews"* (Acts 26:3) because his sister, Bernice, shared her faith with him? The sisters' words of influence in Paul's case may have been spoken alone, at home with their men. Many women, today, wait for just such a time.

Finally, regarding the sisters' exposure to Paul's message of the fulfillment of Messiah in Jesus as the Christ, how do we know how the planted seeds of spirituality grow in anyone's heart? As for all our sisters, may God's seeds of peace and love be planted in every heart and watered daily as we all model and receive God's grace and compassion.

Bernice
Acts 25:13; 25:23; 26:30

Bernice was royalty by birth and by marriage. Her family tree is full of rulers, yet she merely kept them company. It was on one of her companion trips with her brother, King Agrippa II, that she sat in audience to the defense of the Apostle Paul before Porcius Festus. When Paul concluded, Bernice was among those who agreed that Paul should be released, if he had not demanded an audience with Caesar.

Focus Virtue: Mercifulness

*Thus says the LORD of hosts:
Render true judgments,
show kindness and mercy to one another;*

Zechariah 7:9

Tradition tells us that rumors flew when Bernice became the constant companion of her brother, King Agrippa II, after the death of her first husband, who was also her uncle. When her second marriage to the King of Sicily was not successful, and she returned to the companionship of her brother, accusations became even worse. Sometime later, Bernice left the splendor of her royal life and was said to have become a barefooted, hair disheveled, pleader for merciful treatment of the Jews. Neither Bernice nor anyone else can shut out the hurtful words of others, even when wearing royal robes. Most people know what it is like to be hurt by the words or actions of others—and what it is like to be treated mercifully. Mercy is only useful when we freely give it away.

*I will be merciful to others today,
especially if they do not deserve it.*

Drusilla
Acts 24:24

Drusilla, a Jewess, was the younger and more beautiful sister of Bernice. At age 14 Drusilla was married to King Aziz of Emesa, but Felix hired the Cypriote magician Atomus to woo her away from her husband. Drusilla was about 17 years old when she accompanied her second husband, Felix, to his new position as judge—where they would hear the Apostle Paul declare Jesus as the Messiah for two years before they moved on. Tradition says that sometime later, Drusilla died in the eruption of Vesuvius that destroyed Pompeii, along with her six year old son, by Felix.

Focus Virtue: Respectfulness

Pay to all what is due them—taxes to whom taxes are due, revenue to whom revenue is due, respect to whom respect is due, honor to whom honor is due.

Romans 13:7

Drusilla knew what it was like to be a Jewess in a Roman world. To live under Roman rule was not always easy for the Jews, but to live with the Roman ruler must have called for a great deal of respect on the part of Drusilla. She would have had to maintain respect for herself, as well as give due respect to her husband and the Roman rulers over her. We, too, live in two worlds as citizens of this world and Christians who are citizens of the world to come. When we show respect for the rights of others and take care of ourselves and the world around us, we are practicing respectfulness.

Respectfulness means that I am full of respect —for myself, others, and God's creation.

Virtues Reflection: Bernice & Drusilla

Bernice and Drusilla are included in the scriptures for one of more reasons—along with other examples of sisters who were part of biblical history. Bernice and Drusilla are some of the sisters who provide us with examples of Virtues that are worthy of admiration and emulation, as well as being examples of the need to develop and use their Virtues.

When reading, considering, and discussing the stories of these sisters, Bernice and Drusilla, look for examples of the Virtues they could have been using. For example, you may see Bernice using discernment when she concurs with the others that Paul has done nothing worthy of death and could be released had he not appealed to the Emperor. *(You may want to review the Focus Virtues list in Chapter One.)* Identify the Virtues of Bernice and the Virtues of Drusilla. Then complete the following exercise with Bernice and Drusilla in mind.

Which one of the Virtues of Bernice do you most appreciate, today?

Which one of the Virtues of Drusilla do you most appreciate, today?

How have these Virtues been part of your life in the past or in the present?

How do you see these Virtues or the need for them in your life, now?

What can you do to further develop these Virtues in your life?

What has helped you most as a result of this study?

Action Scripture

Luke 6:31-35 *Do to others as you would have them do to you. "If you love those who love you, what credit is that to you? For even sinners love those who love them. If you do good to those who do good to you, what credit is that to you? For even sinners do the same. If you lend to those from whom you hope to receive, what credit is that to you? Even sinners lend to sinners, to receive as much again. But love your enemies, do good, and lend, expecting nothing in return. Your reward will be great, and you will be children of the Most High; for he is kind to the ungrateful and the wicked.*

Grateful Prayer

All Knowing God, it is You who knows our hearts, and the hearts of everyone. Help us to look with love within ourselves and within our sisters to see the goodness, the willingness, and the potential of each of us. We ask to see and to feel Your love within us, now. Let Your love stir within us and reach out to one another to show mercy. We ask that Your Spirit guide us into the Way, the Truth, and the Life that You have for us. Encourage us to see, to be, and to do all the loving acts that we can each day in respectful ways. Grant us grace to follow Your example and to be kind to the ungrateful and the wicked. AMEN

Selected References/Readings

Bellis, Alice Ogden (1994). *Helpmates, Harlots, and Heroes: Women's Stories in the Hebrew Bible.* Louisville, KY: Westminister John Knox.

Bouquet, A.C. (1954). *Everyday Life in New Testament Times.* New York Charles Scribner's Sons.

Bultmann, Rudolf Karl (1971). *The Gospel of John.* Philadelphia: Westminster.

Deen, Edith (1955). *All of the Women of the Bible.* New York: Harper & Row.

Grosvenor, Melville Bell, & Vosburgh, Frederick G. (Eds.) (1967). *Everyday Life in Bible Times.* Washington, D.C.: National Geographic Society.

Harrison, Eveleen (1936). *Little-Known Women of the Bible.* New York: Round Table.

Hollyday, Joyce (1994). *Clothed with the Sun: Biblical Women, Social Justice, and Us.* Louisville, KY: Westminister John Knox.

Karssen, Glen (1975). *Her Name Is Woman.* Colorado Springs, CO: Navpress.

Lofts, Norah (1949). *Women in the Old Testament: Twenty Psychological Portraits.* New York: MacMillan.

Maxwell, Jordan, & Leedom, Tim C. (1993). *The Book Your Church Doesn't Want You to Read.* Lansing, IL: Kendall/Hunt.

McCrum, Robert, Cran, William, & MacNeil, Robert (1986). *The Story of English.* New York: Viking Penguin.

Selected References/Readings continued...

Mead, Frank S. (1934). *Who's Who in the Bible: 250 Bible Biographies.* New York: Harper & Row.

Moltmann-Wendel, Elisabeth (1982). *The Women Around Jesus.* New York: Crossroad.

Nelson, Hazel McCurdy (1958). *Bible Women Come Alive.* New York: Abingdon.

Nunnally-Cox, Janice (1981). *Fore-Mothers: Women of the Bible.* New York: Sebury.

Phipps, William E. (1992). *Assertive Biblical Women.* Westport, CT: Greenwood.

Price, Eugenia (1969). *The Unique World of Women.* Grand Rapids, MI: Zondervan.

Sellier, Charles E., & Russell, Brian (1994). *Ancient Secrets of the Bible.* New York: Dell.

Sessions, Will (1958). *Greater Men and Women of the Bible.* St. Louis, MO: Bethany.

Stanton, Elizabeth Cady (1974, reprint). *The Woman's Bible.* Seattle, WA: Coalition Task Force on Women and Religion.

Tillich, Paul (1955). *The New Being.* New York: Scribner.

Wead, Doug, Lewis, David, & Donaldson, Hal (1982). *Where Is the Lost Ark?* Hampshire, MN: Bethany House.

Wold, Margaret (1987). *Women of Faith and Spirit.* Minneapolis, MN: Augsburg.